Note for Librarians: A cataloguing record for this book is available from Library and Archives Canada at www.collectionscanada.ca/amicus/index-e.html
ISBN 1-4251-0757-5

**PUBLISHING**™
*Offices in Canada, USA, Ireland and UK*

**Book sales for North America and international:**
Trafford Publishing, 6E–2333 Government St.,
Victoria, BC  V8T 4P4  CANADA
phone 250 383 6864 (toll-free 1 888 232 4444)
fax 250 383 6804; email to orders@trafford.com
**Book sales in Europe:**
Trafford Publishing (UK) Limited, 9 Park End Street, 2nd Floor
Oxford, UK  OX1 1HH  UNITED KINGDOM
phone +44 (0)1865 722 113 (local rate 0845 230 9601)
facsimile +44 (0)1865 722 868; info.uk@trafford.com
**Order online at:**
trafford.com/06-2515

10  9  8  7  6  5  4  3  2  1

# Dedication:

This book is dedicated to
Ms. Whoopi Goldberg, *Caryn Johnson*;
Anne Frank for inspiration;
Cyndi Lauper for her voice;
and the teachers – don't forget about them - because without them
we'd be lost in this world;
and anyone else...for you know who you are. Thanks !

# ...And So Am I

This story has been written by someone who has been diagnosed as having schizophrenia, or possibly still schizoaffective disorder that is a combination of things known as mental illness.

Where shall I begin? I guess first I want you to make all your own conclusions with an open mind. I do not intend to change anyone's minds, endorse anyone or anything and the like. Some things may be true, may be dreams, or may be nothing at all. In this journey you may be the judge. You may do whatever it is you wish to do (aside from copying it) but I ask you not to judge people. Everyone's journey is quite different. Some people excel in areas others do not. People make mistakes. Unfortunately, not all words or deeds can be forgiven on this existence on earth. What is right and what is wrong is something that is decided in part by the Norm of society and a higher power of your choice.

The title of this book is an excerpt of a joke that went around when I was in high school. The verse went: Roses are red, violets are blue, I'm schizophrenic, and so am I. I can remember my best friend and I laughed and laughed at that. Maybe we had a warped sense of humor. I still think it is funny. Some of that which I went through a few years later was not. It has however made me much stronger as a person spiritually. Well, at least I think about it a lot more. It is why I am still here. It is why I am writing this.

About three years ago I began to do my usual routine. I had injured both of my wrists at my last job and had a lengthy, messy bout with the insurance company. In a round about way, they got me to see their psychiatrist for a pain evaluation. I knew something was not right. I finished the tests and interviews. I was in a strange daze. As I left the office, I picked up one of the doctor's business cards. His title read psychiatrist-lawyer-forensics expert. I left there so burnt out I couldn't cry...yet. I felt so violated after this testing I went through that day that I vowed I would never go to a psychiatrist again. Somehow, I managed to convince myself that all psychiatrists were somehow like the last one. Everything I could conceive to go wrong seemed to do so. For the first time in my life things seemed out of control.

A few days later after the appointment I felt a cold cutting sensation separate the two halves of my brain. I felt in conflict somehow, kind of confused toward some subjects, but for the most part was just basically tense. At one point, I physically felt the right side of my brain squirming like gelatin.

A religious friend of mine repeatedly told me we were in the end times and basically insisted that I was being oppressed by demons. I was totally oblivious to both of these ideas at first. This was incomprehensible, unreal, and impossible to my mind. Things were for the most part back to normal. I was, however, scared of certain things.

It was certainly time for a change. I was finally awarded $20,000 for a 13.5% permanent impairment of my right hand by the worker's compensation insurance company. I moved to a local city into a second floor studio apartment. I now felt safer than I had in my other apartment. The (persistent) people from the insurance company did not know where I lived. They had stalked me for about a year. It was in this case more than just paranoia. I would occasionally see them watching me. Following me. They always made sure that I saw them though. I think they wanted me to be afraid of them. I was awarded the impairment and all this should be over. It was, but for a little while afterwards I still looked over my shoulder.

...And So Am I

Now came the task of trying to find a new job. I filled out numerous applications for almost a whole year.

About this time, I had bought a newer car that ran well, now that I had some money. I kept my Post Office box in my hometown and frequented a spiritual shop and crystal shop nearby. I found the art and books fascinating and the possibility of the sixth sense drew me in. Spirituality was taught to me somewhat in the church, but was relatively limited. I was never taught that learning was evil, so I tried to keep with what I was taught and supplement it with what I thought was good. I did a great deal of reading on spiritual healing and also that which is usually called ESP, I learned that anything used to help people was good if it worked. If it did not work it was in my opinion not God's will or at least not the will of the person.

I had practiced going back and forth with colors and numbers with a friend who was actually quite gifted. We noticed that some people were able to pick up on things easier that others were. We didn't consider ourselves psychic, yet we were able to some degree pick up on other's controlled thoughts. He was good at numbers. I, being more emotional had a tendency to pick up on colors more easily. I even noticed I could picture the color in my mind in controlled situations.

One other unusual thing happened before I even thought about the healing energies of the universe. I visited the spiritual shop where the owner sold stones commonly called crystals. She was sitting behind the counter with a friend talking. I was looking at the display of crystals trying really hard not to listen to what they were talking about. Then something I will never forget happened. I heard music for a second. It was very beautiful and could be likened to a huge chorus.

I do not know what caused the music. I've tried to come up with some theories. One being the stones somehow allowed me to tune into something like a quartz crystal did in radios at one time or maybe each stone had a different vibration like a subtle version of a guitar string. Maybe they were Angels. I really do not know. I was sensitive to things around me; I just did not understand it, really.

Another thing that was very difficult in my life at this time was my grandmother's failing health. She had had a stroke and could not speak, but would wail as though something was hurting her. She was in the final stages of Alzheimer's disease and was confined to a special chair on wheels. I would go and visit her and would repeat my name until I felt she recognized me. She was usually happy to see me and because she could not speak, she usually would hold my hand. I remember the first time I held her hand I was beginning to be very ill but could manage the symptoms without medication. At times, though I would hold her hand and see a rainbow of colors, which I could feel wash over me and make me feel better. I began to try to talk to her telepathically, as it was proposed in a book I got at a local bookstore. Sometimes she would light up. Occasionally she would run her hand over the left side of her head which correlating with the book might have meant, "listen." I could not hear although at times I thought I could. When I heard anything it was on the right side or so it seemed.

I bought her a teddy bear and put a few small stones in it - in the hope of spiritual healing. I also put a diamond earring on the bear from my own ear. She seemed pleased. I would be strong, and then leave the nursing home in tears. She was very special to me and I wished to communicate with her in some way. I just had a gut feeling that in the years in which she could not speak she was gifted with the things I was studying about but could barely comprehend. The wails continued.

Somehow, one day I got the idea that something was hurting her when she would wail. My illness was getting worse and I began to have bizarre thoughts namely because I now started to believe it was the end of the world. I stopped eating for the most part and was now hearing voices. I got a job at a local grocery store. I elected to quit because along with everything else I couldn't work at their pace. The voices were demeaning to me, starting out slowly then beginning to become more persistent. I began to be confused and see hallucinations. These are alternate reasons why I quit, aside from the physical agony it put on my hands. I never told anyone, I never complained.

One afternoon I was at my parents' house and thought about the wails and the pain my grandmother was obviously in because of the demons. At that point, I was so confused I would have probably done anything to swap places with her. I remember standing in the driveway thinking, "I am young. I can handle this better than she can. I'll try to give her a little peace." I prayed that whatever it was that was hurting her would come to me. I then felt a burning sensation in my lower abdomen. I mean really burning and then, it went away. "That was easy," I thought to myself and I headed towards the post office. All of a sudden, I felt a pop and everything turned red. I literally saw red as though I was wearing red glasses. Things began to get more difficult at this point and the voices and confusion got worse. I got another job, and I remember the physical burning and the "tactile hallucinations" began. At first, it was just during the day. Later it would begin happening at night as well. Thereafter, when I went to visit my grandmother, she did not seem happy to see me. I do not remember ever hearing her wail after that.

Anything is possible I guess. Well, I wanted to tell you firsthand that the feelings and thoughts were real, but as to what was causing them, your guess is as good as mine. You see, I loved her very much. I thought about her constantly at this time. I saw her loved ones slowly give up on her. I would not want that to happen to anyone. As for the demons, they were probably just some forms of tactile hallucination; which means a felt hallucination and some sort of energy closure or blockage causing the burning.

By this time, the schizophrenic side of my life really started to get out of control. Not only was I feeling things but I was also seeing things and making thoughts from fragments of nothing. I would listen to music and hear what was at one time familiar now becoming messages from God or Angels and the like. The opposite also held true. I soon became unable to watch television and other media because of similar effects. Some things would leave me wondering to this day.

One evening I was driving in my car listening to my favorite radio station when I heard static coming through the speakers, cutting off whatever song had been playing. The static then turned into rancid organ music that precluded an eerie dark voice in some unknown language. Coincidentally, as soon as I thought about the inability to understand it, it changed into English. The voice said something to the effect of: "I am Satan. I love pushing your buttons." The voice then called me by name. It then returned to the organ-like music, static and then returned part way through a song in progress. The next couple of days were odd to say the least. I remember once I reached my destination at a local store the alarm went off when I walked through the door.

I later went to a local bookstore to look for something that might explain what was happening to me. I found a book on exorcism and went up to the counter. It rang up wrong. I think the book was supposed to be $5.95 or something. She tried again and it rang up 666. I am not kidding. She laughed and said the book had a mind of it's own. I guess it did.

About this time I was increasingly confused and began to get dizzy. I was still trying to homeopathically or spiritually heal myself and I found myself at the crystal shop.

I told the clerk that I was dizzy and wondered if there was anything that might help. She showed me an inexpensive stone and I figured I would try it. At this point, I could use any help I could get. By this time, I was starting to be avoided as though my illness was visible. I remember the clerk staying away from me as though I was contagious. If I moved closer, she would move away again. Maybe it was just my imagination, simply paranoia.

I could feel my brain moving up and down inside my skull. It was a strange feeling. One side would literally move up and the other would move down. It would be quick. Almost pulsating.

Now I was beginning to get desperate for help. The only problem was that when someone suggested a solution it seemed wrong or I simply did not see what should be done. Sometimes I did what someone suggested. The Bible however, caused hallucinations and abnormal thoughts. Also church and anything religious was difficult. It seemed like the things I loved the most were turning on my in some way. I could not concentrate. A religious friend suggested that I try praying. I taped a circle (for protection) on the floor of my apartment and began to pray pretty much on a much regular basis. One time when I was praying, I heard a scream, a screech in my head that made me want to stop and yet pray harder at the same time.

Every moment became an eternity. I had the voices, confusion, dizziness, random chaotic thinking, the burning, and the poking, the phantom raping, and an eating disorder resulting in a general lack of hygiene. I did not want to leave the house. I thought that because it was the end of the world that food, money, and that which I had collected as material wealth had become evil to me. I went through my apartment and collected almost everything including an extensive tape and CD collection. Also included in the toss were books, videotapes including approximately 80 to 90% of my possessions gone. This did not help.

I pulled some of the things I put out for garbage back inside but I felt uneasy. There was no pleasure in material goods. My wonderful sister told me to keep everything or give them to her for safekeeping. I got scared again and into the garbage and dumpsters it went. I did save some of it this time. Sadly, that which I deemed as evil went into numerous receptacles around town as not to tempt any lost soul. I guess that people are in fact much more important than material goods. In the future when I began to get a little better, I was told by my sister and friends not to worry that it could all be replaced. It just takes time. That which I could not replace I learned I really did not need anyway. To deal with this particular situation I have over time, replaced what I have been able to and have, when and where appropriate, forgotten that it was gone in the first place. This was one of my life's hardest lessons; but at the time, it was something that probably made me stronger as a person.

Still being scared of psychiatrists, I tried to get help from a family practioner. I had an appointment and told her about what was going on as best I could. She had me make a follow up appointment and left it at that. It was one of the longest two weeks of my life.

I lost my job at a local clothing store when I could not fake it anymore and get out of bed one morning. I was running out of money and asked my parents if I could move back home. At this point, I did not care much about pride. I noticed when I had spent the night at my parent's house that the phantom raping was less severe, and sometimes left me alone. I felt safer.

I began packing what was left of my belongings and fit it all in my father's truck as opposed to the multiple vehicles I needed the last time I moved.

Still feeling the end was near; I got a job at a grocery store stocking shelves third shift. I was trying to think about what I could do without thinking much and figured this was a possibility. I could not keep up. My hands hurt so badly from the repetition and the former injuries but I stayed with it as long as I could.

I noticed a resemblance at this point, one day on my break that my symptoms were like that of a television special I once saw on schizophrenia.

The other employees seemed to think that my condition was funny and would make sly remarks and have fun with it often times. I still did not realize that I was sick. Symptoms -- yes. I knew something was not right but since the physician did not do anything, I thought at times it was a normal part of the end times.

One day I began to hallucinate really bad and my hands and knees hurt from stocking. I could not take any more jokes; I could not keep up. I was miserable. Almost in tears, I quit. That was the first time I ever had to quit a job and I will never forget how it felt.

...And So Am I

The voices for the most part told me I should kill myself. I kept fighting it. The doctor I had gone to called to check up on me. She said she did not want to give me medication, which she was not familiar with. She said she did not want to kill me. I was not doing well dealing with the voices.

A few days later, although I had no money to pay for it, I went to the emergency room at a local medical center. I waited for the doctor. Once again I had to explain as much as I could. I remember him looking at me funny. Perhaps it was just me. I told him of the experiences I had and a new symptom of not being able to stop moving. I had the constant need to walk in circles and pace.

He prescribed to me a couple of medications and referred me to a mental health clinic, which would charge you on your ability to pay.

I made an appointment and waited for about four weeks. I was staying at my parents' but was still paying rent until the end of the month. The day of the appointment came and I hoped for the best. They asked me where I was living. I gave them my address. They must have asked for a telephone number where I could be reached because somehow it came out that I was staying at my parents. The clinic turned me away. They said they were overbooked and then referred me to a place about a half an hour away from my parent's house.

I was feeling very ill but the medications seemed to be helping me get by. I had another two-week wait to see the psychiatrist. I was still leery, and with the constant shuffle, I was beginning to believe that maybe, I was not supposed to see anyone. Maybe I was supposed to act on the voices.

I got another job pouring coffee to help pay for the doctor bills and the medications. It was almost time to see the psychiatrist and the medications that were prescribed from the emergency room were refilled with a little reluctance after I explained what had been going on. I took the sedative before work, which helped me for the most part to get by. I worked there three part-time shifts before the visit to the psychiatrist.

The big day arrived and I was nervous but the symptoms were so active that I really did not notice. My first recollection of this day was talking to the psychiatrist and I remember that I could not sit down. I kept standing up and pacing between visits to the chair. I felt as though I could not sit down. My body wanted to move. And besides, it hurt to sit down because I had lost so much weight and the strength went with it. I do not remember our conversation, but I do remember him dialing a number and saying, "Do you have a bed?" After he got his answer he hung up the telephone and told me that I was to go to the hospital. He was very nice; my fear had been pointless. He wrote down directions. I left for the hospital without stopping for my clothes, etc.

# The Mental Health Unit

Iarrived at the hospital within a half an hour and walked into the emergency room waiting area as instructed. I waited there for about an hour before being given a hospital identification bracelet and taken to another room before I was accompanied or escorted up the stairs. The man who stayed with me for most of the time in this room offered me a glass of orange juice and then took me upstairs to the MHU.

I do not remember exactly what happened next, but I remember being shown to my room with another man who kept screaming for medication. I then saw a doctor who told me I was having an allergic reaction to the anti-psychotics and changed my medication. (I do not know however if I was having any reaction because the symptoms were the same as they had been anyway.) Then they put me to bed. The hospital bed was very hard and it made it even harder to sleep than it already was. Somehow, I got a prescription for a foam mattress. They gave me horse-pills to get me to sleep.

I paced the hallway repeatedly and had a cigarette every chance I got. I just had to find the person with the matches. (We were not allowed to have belts, dental floss, or lighters, etc. but we could have people walking around with matches.)

The first few days were miserable and they kept trying to get me to sleep. Eventually, it became a little easier and the tests started coming. I had blood tests, a CT scan, and agonizing personality tests. I met with all kinds of mental health professionals who gave me even more tests. My memory was still very bad and I remember fighting to remember things. I could not remember the names of the nurses most of the time.

The activities began as optional at first. I had to attend art sessions and group therapy sessions. There was usually a card game going and they kept trying to get me to play.

I remember not being able to fill out my menu request and having to have a nurse help me fill it out. I was now making myself eat and trying to get my mind back on track. It was not easy. I had to let go of the past as the best I could at the time in order to survive in the mental health environment.

I want to say that this hospital stay was possible the worst and best time of my life.

The medication screamer was discharged and I had my own room for a while; he left me some of his clothes. Around my second or third day, a new patient came to the hospital. She had earrings up and down her ears and was admitted for attempting to take too many pills. She later became a friend, which I still have to this day. Her name is Dawn. I saw her a lot because she was in the room across from the smoking room.

About this time, I was sent to see the social worker. I had been fighting many emotional problems and still had not forgotten the bad stuff that had happened; the demons among them. As I was talking to the social worker I felt a surge of energy being sent to me, which sent me into a frenzy. He told me something along the lines of "Don't worry, I'm a professional," but I still freaked out and cried alone in my room for the rest of the day. I was given a pill that knocked me out. Unfortunately, I did not trust him at all after that. It was something that might not bother normal people, but it scared the crap out of me. I did not feel safe anymore. I had to pretend. I had to deal.

Among the many activities that went on were our daily or semi-daily walks to the outside world. I was beginning to become less tolerant to the outside world, so this was a therapy. Another incentive was that we could smoke as many cigarettes as we wanted while we were walking. This was opposed to the one per visit in the smoking room. It was greatly looked forward to by me probably more than any of the other activities.

On my first day and the day I flipped-out I was put on safety watch and not allowed to leave the MHU.

My memory is a bit fuzzy but among the activities were field trips to the store or other quiet places on back roads. We also went to a bowling alley and a Native American POW-WOW that scared me overall. At the Native American show, I bought some rocks. One of the schizophrenics was a Native American and was really into this assembly. He would explain to us what was going on and told us what some of the ceremony meant. He had however, a really bad temper and was easily upset over what others might consider the littlest things. He did have a big heart and bought gifts for some of us. This was a small group.

He was my roommate for a while until he freaked out really bad and they separated us so I would be safe from his violent mood swings.

Somewhere about this time on 4/7/95, I wrote a short poem. I had written many in the past but thought I had lost that part of me to the illness. I still am unsure how I was able to write this at the time but I am glad I did. Here it is, I hope you like it.

*What these eyes have seen,*
*What the body felt –*
*I'm not alone somehow*
*(regrets expense paid in full)*
*Those who know,*
*Those who pull –*
*Forward, slightly forward*
*Take a step each day –*
*Hope to find a foothold,*
*Make it on my way.*

...And So Am I

I remember vaguely walking around a department store with Dawn by my side comforting me as I chronically freaked out. This is when I bought some socks. This was actually a significant time in my life as strangely as that sounds.

At the bowling alley, I was not freaking out as badly but I was seriously sedated and remember wondering how I was supposed to knock down any of the pins. I guess I did but I do not really remember. All I remember was that I did not have the lowest score although we were not playing for points.

At one of the field trips we went to a video store and rented movies. I can only remember one of them, one that I believe I helped pick out. I remember most of us sitting in the day room. I was very fidgety still and was extremely sensitive to subject matter. I remember trying to sit still and then giving up. I would pace back and forth between the doorway and the couch and then back into the hallway. I really do not remember what bothered me but in retrospect, it was probably violent themes and the possibility or the occurrence of hallucinations.

I still shouted "STOP" repeatedly out loud as a means of stopping the voices and irrational thoughts. This is something I did now without realization that I was doing it.

Somehow, I was now managing to do my laundry and fill out my daily menu requests. I now had clean underwear (I refused to wear a hospital gown) as friends and family brought me things I needed. One item I really wanted was dental floss. You could never realize how much you missed something until it was taken away. We were like small children in some ways. I was allowed to floss my teeth but had to return the used floss to the front desk.

After I became somewhat stable I was allowed to shave, which I was for some reason unlike the others, allowed to do so by myself. I still paced.

One afternoon on returning from one of our walks we all got into the elevator. The button was pushed and we began moving. Then the elevator stopped. We waited for a few minutes then a man called for help. The man who did the calling was more agitated and upset than the group from the walk. One in the group was hyperventilating and the man on the telephone told the people on the other end that this girl was having a heart attack. Eventually, we were rescued without any heart attacks. We took the stairs for a while.

It is now that I am going to get into something that changed my life. It is something I could never forget. This happened between a week, and a week and a half into my three-week stay. As I mentioned earlier I was very sensitive to my surroundings and I heard messages and saw visions at the same time I was hallucinating. This may be important to remember here. Although for reasons to be stated I believe this to be true with all my heart I will leave you the benefit of doubt.

I was at this time at odds with God. I tried like anything to stay humble but I was really loosing sight of my religious outlook. I remembered Jesus and accepted him as best I could as a great man who lived. I began saying, "Stop it, Jesus" and later shortened it to "Jesus." Anyway, I was really for the first time in my life almost atheist. I hope He understands this. On with the show.

I smoked a cigarette and left the smoking room. I probably paced the hallways a few times. I stopped outside Dawn's room (the rooms were not co-ed) and I went into shock. Instead of seeing Dawn or her roommate, I saw the form of a man with long blond hair lying in Dawn's bed. His face was barely visible but was that of a man. The form was relatively stiff looking. I told no one but a nurse. She told me not to tell anyone about it.

This made me think and reason. Maybe God was trying to tell me something. I took it as a sign and basically left it at that. I felt less alone. I was chosen by a spirit to view him. I thought that if spirits were real, then there must be angels, and if there were angels then there definitely was a God. Everything seemed to make sense. Everything is made of atoms on this material plane. Atoms are made of energy. Energy is love. Spirits and angels are energy. The light went on in my head.

...And So Am I

The next night I was woken up by shouting early in the morning. Dawn was in my doorway calling my name. The nurses came running, but I was awake and I heard Dawn say, "There is a ghost in my bed." Why she came to me is a mystery. She said that a voice told her that I would understand. This is when Dawn and I really became friends. This was not the last of the ghost. I never saw him again but I felt his presence and sometimes I heard him following flashes of green light between my hallucinations.

For me it was difficult to tell the difference between message and hallucination. Nevertheless, the fact remains that Dawn who was not schizophrenic sometimes heard messages, the same messages as myself; this I found quite impressive. He told Dawn his name was Sam. He would not tell us how he died. He told me he needed to eat (literally) to stay in his state of being. He gave us encouragement and played tricks on us to remind us he was there.

One morning in particular I remember mentally telling Sam he could have some of my food if he wanted. My coffee dropped about a half an inch as though being sucked out by a straw, to my amusement. The showers would turn off and on by themselves. Whenever I began to doubt something extraordinary would happen.

I guess one day that I was thinking to myself that it was hallucinations or delusions that I was experiencing as part of my illness. I forgot easily at this point. This particular morning I had a new personal plastic coffee mug (how I loved coffee). I was sitting across from the nurse who I had originally confided in. She was very nice and was not openly judgmental about it. I guess she thought it was possible after all. Anyway, this morning Sam was up to his tricks and moved my filled coffee mug approximately six inches across the table. I looked up at the nurse and asked her if she saw it. Just as I was asking her the mug moved again, this time without a doubt she saw it. She gave me a smile. I did not tell anyone about it. This time I knew beyond a doubt that there was a Sam. I love him as a friend to this day.

...And So Am I

The rest of my stay was basically routine. They kept adding additional days to my stay. I got a new roommate who was also schizophrenic. He hardly talked and smiled all the time. He made me nervous. I got into an argument with one of the nurses because she said Dawn and I were sitting too close on the couch. She came in and made me move. I told her what I thought of her. This was the only time I had any signs of a temper. It was justifiably so. I told her that I was going to report her to the others. She was a temporary worker. She liked Dawn an awful lot though, and I'm not kidding around.

I was granted personal leaves from the hospital in which I was petrified but I pulled through. I got a pair of sandals on one trip on foot to the (far, far away) downtown. I remember thinking about passing out. Upon going to the bank, I did not know how to act or what to say. I was so drugged up. Dawn left three days before I did. We exchanged telephone numbers and addresses and promised to keep in touch.

Then came my day to go home. I got many hugs and address which although I wrote; the effort was never reciprocated. I guess they all wanted to forget the past.

# Small Steps up the Mountain Path

**17 Feb. 1997**

I find myself struggling between how much I should weigh and what and how much I should eat. I have a tendency towards bingeing when I do eat, but when I don't eat usually I go almost all day without eating. I am finding this troublesome because I want to work out at the local gym. I however have to eat to do this. I weigh almost my "ideal" weight. I am afraid of gaining unwanted weight as opposed to muscle. Secretly, and for some unknown reason I still think I should weigh what I did in high school (approximately 135 lbs.). I feel guilty that I have over the last seven years gained about twenty pounds. I must eat. I have to consciously eat, or I will not. I know it helps my situation but I honestly am not sure as to the extent. I feel stronger when I eat, yes. I have gained muscle, yes. I can stand and sit without it hurting, yes. I guess it is good to eat but still...

I would like to get into modeling again. Unfortunately, for the reasons that may be a gut is not usually a salable attribute or "control point" as it was explained to me. There are exceptions to almost any rule. I guess I feel that in acting the salability is a little better. I guess that along with most of the population I would like to look like the people in the posters at the gym.

Why don't you just lift weights, etc.? Well, I do but it does not seem to do much, and because of my wrists I cannot do much lifting,

...And So Am I

hence I'm back to eating again. I know that the weight I have gained has done more good than harm. I will try to remember that.

I felt the burning last night. As with any of the symptoms they have been greatly diminished with the regular consumption of my medications. I do not remember offhand how often I feel it, but I would say it has been very subtle and for the most part reasonably acceptable.

My mind has been very sensitive lately, especially on the right side. I do not hear any voices but maybe a low buzzing sound that varies in pitch when it is quiet. It may be part of my illness but I wish to believe it to be something of ESP at least to keep me going. I have been feeling a lot of energy lately especially around my naval area. A book I read said there were different colors associated with different areas of the body. This energy would be orange.

A dilemma I have is, where is this energy coming from? An Angel? A spirit? A higher power, or just a human being who is strong in telepathy or other healing ways? Anyhow, they always seem to comfort me with this energy when I start to get sick.

I have been seeing colors still with my eyes closed, and sometimes see purple at night or in shadows. It used to bother me (why can't I be normal?) but now I find the purple to be comforting. There is definitely a distinct difference between the colors and hallucinations. There is also a difference between good and bad voices. Unfortunately, though when one is not in a sound state of mind, the two can be entwined and I could not tell the difference between the schizophrenic and other states of mind. I have always been sensitive but I do not believe that I have always been sick. The medications I take numb both sides of my brain. I am also well enough now to know that there is a difference and I use my discretion to discriminate between the two. One problem with this is the fact that when I get sick or a symptom surfaces it makes me have a harder time deciphering between the two. I would love to be able to say I am at a point where I know the difference but I honestly tell you that sometimes I do not. I just do not act upon the voices, which in my opinion is my only option.

I meditate to try to relax but it is not a sure thing that anything will happen or that good will come as a result. At the same time I wish to grow spiritually and evolve as a human being if that is what was meant for me. I do not give in, but I also have not given up. This writing is in part to prove that. I am functional for the most part in my present routine. I have been told that some people with schizophrenia are kept locked up. I have been very lucky in that respect. I will not forget it.

On the manic side of my illness, the medicines have also been proven very helpful. I have been depressed twice in the last week but have been able to get out of it. Before this medication was prescribed (the anti-manic), I was having a good day, bad day thing going. I was not violent externally but on the inside, I wanted to inflict pain on myself. My reasoning was to take away from the mental pain for a while. Physical pain seemed to dull the frustration of the mental plane. As usual I tried to use caution when feeling out of control and only acted on this urge to harm myself physically once in this way. The anti-manic also controlled my suicidal thoughts to some degree. It has for the most part evened out my moods, which has helped me to heal on a mental level.

There are the things that I will never forget, but when your mind functions pretty normally the bad things don't repeat over and over like a CD player on repeat. It could be stupid little things; random thoughts. My memory has also improved tremendously over the last couple of years. I still have a hard time remembering things but I remember well enough that most things make sense and are not as confusing as they were once.

Since my doctor took me off the anti-depressant my stress has changed. I still have the same amount of stress, but it seems to be less overwhelming and now tends to creep up on me. It builds but the stress medication makes it tolerable, usually.

The side effects of the medications can be frustrating. I accept them as being part of the illness. They are however, minuscule compared to what I went through before.

Every once in a while or when it decides to surface I get a (usually) milder version of the symptom as a reminder. How often? I take it as something usual, so I couldn't tell you, exactly. I usually only remember when it gets intolerable; I feel out of control or scared. Usually one will follow another. Thankfully, I have a great support network, which has helped me to be the person I am now. I accept the things I cannot change and change that which I can. I pray to know the difference.

Tonight I am lonely and anxious. I am feeling rather spaced out. The loneliness is not new. It is something that cannot usually be filled by anyone. It somehow goes beyond that kind of loneliness. It is a desire; an outreach that can only be filled with thoughts of God. It is something that has helped me through my rough times. In the hospital I was taught to say "stop," when I had voices or irrational or uncontrollable thoughts. I added "Jesus" on my own. I have probably said it a million times or more. It has helped. God was much too vast of a topic; Jesus was a little more personal. I wanted the powers that be to know that I didn't blame them for my anguish and that I was at least trying to remember them above all else. It can be a difficult task. I have been told that I may never be normal again. This is hard to take. I haven't given up hope.

I am not sure why I am so fidgety tonight. I took a nap earlier today, but I am still tired. Sometimes I begin to shake. I am a little shaky now but it is not that bad. I took my meds and am waiting for the peace it brings.

What did I do today? Well, I woke up to the sound of my mother waking my siblings up for school. It feels like I am up too early. I have always been a second shift person until I got sick. Since it was snowing, my mother asked me to bring the "kids" to school. Upon arriving at the school my sister hands me some money from my mother to buy myself a coffee. (I love coffee) I save the money and return home. I make myself some coffee and take a shower. I decide to get dressed up today for the ladies at a local nursing home where I volunteer for a couple of hours every Monday. I arrive at the home and make conversation with the staff and other volunteers when possible. This was partly frustrating today because the employees were extremely busy; and the social differences between the other volunteers and myself made it difficult at times to socialize.

Since my illness (and probably before) I have kept much to myself. I am trying hard to fit into society. I have been told I seem arrogant. I must say this is one thing I seriously do not believe to be true. A teacher told me this. Since it was a modeling instructor, I will say it would be safe to assume that my body language might have leaned this way. Honestly, if he really knew me he would not have made the remark. I speak when spoken to. I rarely start a conversation. I have tried to be a little more talkative, though. My personal thoughts of it is too cold out today has been socially translated into it is beautiful out today a little cold but nice out; that sort of thing. I have been in a way brushing up on my acting skills. At first, it was not easy to act chipper when I did not feel very well.

I do not watch much media other than movies for the most part. I really don't like the news or newspapers much at all. This makes it even harder to be social. I tend to think more locally such as issues at home or work that directly affects me. Not intending to sound negative, the media is quite redundant and does not seem to serve much purpose but to fill heads with garbage in need of recycling.

Back to the volunteer part. Growing up with three sisters, having a former girlfriend whom was a beautician and modeling class got me into doing my girlfriends fingernails. I am not a professional but that is what I do every Monday morning. I enjoy doing it. Would I want to do it professionally? Probably not. Three hours is enough for me. Today was slow. I only had three women come down to the activity room only one of which was a regular. I love to talk to the women. Sometimes, if I'm lucky, they will look and tell me I did a good job. I am not fast, but I try hard to do a good job. It pays off. Sometimes they expect me to charge them money. The women then look shocked or ask again when I tell them I am a volunteer. Painting nails has given

...And So Am I

me a sense of accomplishment and socialization. I found that if you keep it real when you speak to the residents they would really have a conversation with you. They like to hear what you've been up to. After a person knows someone and trusts him or her, there is the ability to speak freely. Before they know you, there is the usual test the boundaries conversation. You as a person can turn a conversation around for the better. I had great teachers in life.

I go back home. I rest for an hour then write for an hour. I then give in and eat. One of my favorite things in the world is going to the post office to check my mailbox. Nothing, but that is okay. I go back home and sleep for about two hours. I wake up and do not feel refreshed. I go downstairs and keep busy while I wait for it to be time to go to my play rehearsal.

I go to rehearsal and remember my lines for the first part of the play covered. I notice that one of the cast is missing and became worried that she might be seriously sick. Probably just my imagination, but it stays with me. I go back home and want desperately to sleep but my brother is in our room doing his homework. And so I write.

The medication is beginning to take effect and I am beginning to calm down. I can't wait for tomorrow; good night.

## 18 Feb 1997

My emotions for the most part at the present are external. I physically feel emotions. It is a detachment of some sort. I do feel. I guess that I just have to think about it and rationalize what I should be feeling. It can be and is at times confusing, but I just say to myself, "Okay, this is what I am feeling," now what do I think about this person. It is not limited to anyone in particular. It is similar to, but is not a sexual feeling. It does not come from the groin not burn. However, it can be felt as a similar energy. It is like being colorblind emotionally. It definitely is not orange (usually). I seem to be able to tell if a person truly cares about me by this means. It does not mean that when I don't feel it they do not care. Everyone is different. It took me some pain to learn this.

Maybe they are at a different spiritual level than myself. With some, I believe we have been friends before our birth. I don't really know. Maybe our souls are speaking to one another. I guess that is how I would like to think of this. We always try to find a rational answer for everything. Have you ever noticed that? I think that it is in our nature to rationalize. Some things do not have an answer they just are. I believe that one-day we will understand it all.

Other times I have a deep longing as a baby has for his mother. I believe this is internal. This is however the same feeling with a different intensity at different times for different people.

### 28 Feb. 1997

Good morning everyone. It is early yet for me to be up, and I still have a few hours before I have to be at work.

While I was having a cigarette, I was thinking. I guess I do that from time to time. I noticed that although being far from perfect, the medications have controlled the up and downs (depression, anger, the desire for self mutilation and the euphoric spells) to give me at least an illusion of what I believe to be normal. I am however still experiencing the fact that "down" follows "up" or a "crash" as I call it has been happening again. I have noticed recently that I was in an excellent mood, feeling pretty normal and that night I crashed hard. I didn't know what to do so I took a sedative that was prescribed for panic attacks. The anxiety follows or accompanies the bad mood; the sedative takes away part of the anguish. It usually calms me down enough so that I can handle the situation on my own.

Sometimes, however it does not work as I had hoped it would and I tear up, curl into a ball on my bed, and wait for it to pass. Sometimes I wait to pass out from my medication. The usual suggestions by the medical establishment usually do not help. I do call the help line on occasion to let them know what is going on. Oftentimes, it is good just to talk to someone who is supposed to know how to help.

It does pass. I try to keep it on my own. I do and always will appreciate all the midnight hour telephone calls they accepted and all the calls returned to help me out.

## 31 Mar. 1997

Yesterday was Easter Sunday. It was a rough day for the most part. I woke up early to find the Easter Bunny still remembered me. I was side tracked and tried to concentrate on the tasks at hand. The television was on and all that was on was religious services and singing. Although I was not too terribly in a bad mood; for obvious reasons earlier stated I had a hard time dealing with the "Church" issues today.

Others in the house aside from my mother were scurrying about so, in an effort to escape, I went into the living room. The television was still on and my mother being moved by the sermon encouraged me to join her. I listened for a little while and then lost all interest. I felt like a rat in a maze for the beginning of the morning.

I was scheduled to work the morning shift at the movie theatre so I put my uniform on (black pants and a white shirt) haphazardly put on a tie and put my increasingly demeaning bow tie in my pocket.

I drove myself to the church since I had to go immediately to work following the mass. I parked my car and was told to move it. I moved it and was told once again to move it so other members of the parish could park. I got out and inspected my parking job and concretely decided that any of my parking spots were okay. When I left the church others had parked where I had been. This obviously did not give me Easter cheer when I knew deep down that I needed it.

Usually my mood is okay in the morning and gets increasingly worse as the day progresses. This is not always the case. The medications have somewhat broken this pattern. Unfortunately, today it was not the case.

We wait in the church from 30 to 45 minutes before the mass even begins. I was already physically and mentally uncomfortable but my sister asked if there was anything that she could do to help. That in itself did help for a little while. It seemed in my brain that someone actually listened when I said I was uncomfortable and a little scared. Usually I don't feel this. I was grateful.

The service begins with a chorus of men and women and a group of guitar players. I kept praying to Jesus to help me through this. I tried to clear my mind but it kept alternating between both sides of my brain until I noticed and obvious pull to the right side. This upset me because I loose control with that side. It is hard to concentrate. I kept my eyes closed for nearly the whole hour except for when I was supposed to kneel, sit or stand.

It is now time for communion. I am very self-conscious. I am wearing my work uniform and have long hair that I have only trimmed since I got out of the hospital. I have earrings in my left ear. I have rings on each finger of my left hand, which are like badges. I decided this was who I was and that God would understand. I decided to myself that it didn't matter.

Upon leaving the church, I walked up to the priest who was smiling and shaking hands wishing them a happy Easter. When I approached him he lost his smile and merely exchanged the statement. Okay, I tried. I am not perfect. I hope the powers that be love me in long hair, rings and all. I try to believe it.

I left feeling very sad. Tears were not falling but I felt like I was about to cry. Okay, I know that I am not a regular churchgoer, but didn't I deserve a smile when I left? When I am at work it is my job to be friendly. I try to accept everyone and do my best to greet everyone.

Perhaps, because of my illness, I have blown the whole thing out of proportion. I do not intend to disrespect the church in any way. I have a great respect for the churches. I guess maybe they're just not for me.

I begin to cry, briefly. I couldn't let out my feelings. I stopped almost as soon as I began.

I arrive at work. I am early and am sitting on the sidewalk chain smoking. I go inside and use the pay phone to wish a friend a happy Easter. I punch in and then curl up behind the counter waiting for the day; to begin. I was conscious but wished I was not.

The day was excruciatingly slow and I had not eaten because of the mass. I also didn't have any extra money to spare. I usually don't. I was missing dinner with my family. As the day progressed, I was not feeling any better. I have been at this same job for two years with only a few mistakes and one sick day. I wanted very badly to quit. I am not someone who just gives up, but sometimes you have to leave the nest. In this respect I believe I am outgrowing this job.

They send me home early due to the lack of work. I go upstairs and take a sedative and try to sleep. I get up, feel a little better and go eat a plate my mother had prepared for me.

I miss an old girlfriend and call around to find out when we could meet (No, nothing is going on, by the way). I see her Easter evening. I felt better at this point. We watch a video, laugh a bit and thus concludes my Easter Sunday 1997.

## 31 Mar. 1997

Today I am having trouble with the here and now. A kind of longing for things that I had in life and either outgrew or lost. I miss my grandparents and can't believe they are "gone" or better yet I have forgotten that and then had to remember. I miss the eighties and the music of that era. Reoccurring, along with the new, everything seems old or used and gives little comfort. I guess that is my problem today. I will do my best to keep my chin up although it is rough today.

Despite personal talents, I cannot feel any self worth tonight. Good night.

My sister just came in and brushed my hair aside and told me that I had nice hair. Thank you, I really needed that.

**29 Apr. 1997**

Well, I have decided that the job at the theatre was getting me nowhere. I applied at a video store near my house and was hired yesterday. As I began this new journey, I was intensely aware of my illness. There were so many numbers to memorize and I had to remember commands on the computer. I guess it will become easier with time if I make it. I say this because there is a one-month trial period. I left feeling extremely overwhelmed.

Sometimes I think too much and feel as though I am so sober that it hurts. This does not necessarily mean a lack of alcohol or such, but does cause much pain. I guess it is MY pain.

I am actually still working at the theatre for two more weeks and although I can do the work I am uneasy and dreading going in. My boss at the theatre told me that he would put me on the schedule any time I wanted or needed work. Therefore I have some job security after all.

Recently, I painted a picture of Disney's Prince from Beauty and the Beast. I also drew a pencil sketch of my favorite actress. I was pleased with the outcome yet they always seem imperfect and unfinished in some way. This also holds true for my writing and poetry. They never seem to be done, although I am learning to let go and say, "Yeah, that's about right" and let it be at that.

I have been very self-conscious possibly because I feel so sober. I have been put on a different antidepressant, but I am not sure that it is doing much. I know that it gives me anxiety. I remember being giddy for the first few days off and on between the anxiety attacks; but that is about it. A little better possibly, but not much.

This leads me to my gym membership. I have not been going. I am very awake and the "self-conscious" thing has possibly caused me not to feel good about going. There are other things as well but as for now I will not get into that.

Because my symptoms are coming back or have not left (I'm not really sure which) the woman at the financial aid for school says that

...And So Am I

she will not back me up at this time. She said my instability would make school difficult and in turn school would make my life difficult. You get the picture. Will I ever be ready for school?! This left me hurt but relieved because new challenges are always scary. I was willing to give it a shot. I am good at following through with what I set out to do. I have a tendency of letting things run me into the ground. I usually don't give up on the task at hand. When it comes to myself that is a different story. It is just who I am.

On the positive side, I have been comforted lately by the person or spirit, Powers that Be or whomever it is that comforts (or tries to) me. When I have been upset it sends me orange healing energy. It also seems to try to warn me of stress or problems that I am overlooking somehow. I give thanks.

When and where will I fit in?

## 16 May 1997

Well, it has been about a month now and as usual a lot has transpired. I started a new job, although I am not happy with it as I thought I would be. I saw the psychiatrist and she changed my medicine to control the manic depression or crashes, which had been becoming more frequent, again. So far, since I have been on this new drug, I have not crashed! I am still fidgety or agitated and possibly a little depressed.

I seem to be thinking a little clearer the past couple of days; hopefully it will last.

The new job consists of computer work (in which I am basically illiterate) and a lot of busy work including kissing up to the customers. I believe in courteousness and friendliness but this job is downright miserable for me. I needed a change and that is what I got. My old boss still wants me to work for him. I don't mind. At least I have job security if that is how I am to look at it.

Today I got another job offer. The local nursing home where I volunteer is looking for help in the kitchen. I am thinking that maybe I will take this job ($2.00 more an hour, too) and work a night here and there at the movie theatre. This way I would have two good jobs and get to see free movies.

## 03 June 1997

The new drug is working on my mood changes and is doing a pretty good job. I am however, very physically tired from the combination of medications. I am finding it extremely difficult to find motivation. I am tired almost all the time. All I want to do is sleep, but that option is not very productive. I don't want to loose my job but I am afraid that I will just blow it off because I am too tired. This will probably never happen but still, I worry all the same.

Today for some unknown reason I have been given the opportunity to fight depression. I was feeling a little scattered earlier and now I must conquer this symptom. On the whole I feel a lot better than I have for a while but I wonder still if I will ever feel normal or at least, what I consider it to be.

## 15 June 1997

I feel as if I am being mocked by the world. Either that or I am mocking the world.

## 17 June 1997

Today I am left feeling like I let everyone down. I quit smoking cigarettes for twelve consecutive days. I went back because of the mental stress. I got over the physical addiction. I am getting a mixed response. My mother was very upset and left me feeling guilty. I figured that I would quit again tomorrow, but after talking with my psychiatrist, she said she would prefer it if I didn't quit right now. My case manager explained to me that nicotine seems to control some of the "affective" symptoms that I have. You have to weigh everything and then which way do you choose? I am finding this to be a very difficult decision to make. I will quit, but should I wait? To whom should which reason be justified? Is my comfort an issue? The reasons against smoking are quite obvious to me. I know it is a ticket to health problems. I know this. What do you do when all the reasons turn out to be about equal? I guess I have to pick a side. Can you understand the torment this presents? I guess it is a matter of when I will quit.

Today I also discussed with the doctor some of the things that I have been experiencing lately. Lack of motivation is one thing. Also, small bouts with depression that leave me very weak or unstable usually last about a day or two. I addressed the fact that I have been less tired since she cut my dose of the neuroleptic medication. (anti-psychotic) Lastly, I discussed my being scared a lot of the time. I am still functioning though for the most part. I don't like the paranoia all the same. An example of this would be a fear of getting in my car and going to work. It is not necessarily either the driving, the work or both. It is hard to explain. I am able to overcome this for the most part; but I do not like the feeling all the same. I inquired about an anti-depressant that supposedly has had some success at helping people quit smoking. I am still thinking about quitting, you see.

### 18 June 1997

Well, today I smoked but I didn't really feel much like it. Tomorrow I plan to try to quit again. I really don't feel much better either way so I might as well try again.

Something extraordinary happened yesterday. As stupid as it sounds, it made me feel good. As I was driving my car, a lady leaned out of her car and said, "Hey, baby." I know it is childish, but it was a good ego trip.

### 19 June 1997

Today began as usual. Nothing really good, but not terribly bad either. As the day progressed I slowly became stressed out. I was uncomfortable, so I took a half a tablet of my stress medication as a PRN (take as needed) and had an anticipated hour wait yielding results. I was then put on the euphoric side of my manic illness. This may or may not have anything to do with the med. The medication itself does not cause euphoria; but the relief may have caused this to happen. Anyway, I am writing about it because I am "crashing" or reality is setting in and I am frustrated that I have nothing to do to fit my mood. It is as though people around me are not in the same existence as I am and it is bringing me down. The medication that I take for this part of my disorder is still pretty much working. Hence, this writing. When I used to crash, I felt uncomfortable doing anything. I can see that this medication is doing a lot of good. I would recommend this medication to a friend with the disorder. It has minimal side effects and relatively good results. Life is not easy for me, but I will say that it is of higher quality now.

**27 June 1997**

It is not uncommon for me to feel like doing something, anything, but not having the drive to even pick up a book or watch television. This is how I spend a great deal of my time. I want to do something, but feel uncomfortable in doing so. Right now I am waiting for time to pass so I can call my sister in California.

Sometimes things are good after I start them but usually I don't get the enjoyment out of the task as I remember or expect. This is ultimately one of my biggest problems, which I do not believe can be aided with medication. I have been up for over two hours and still haven't done anything. At four o'clock I go to work, but for now, I am alone in the house with my unmotivativeness.

I still don't have much self-esteem. I don't know if I will ever get that back. I haven't hallucinated lately, actually for quite some time. I am however, unhappy with the side effects of the anti-psychotic. This then leads me back to self worth. I won't get into specifics, but one of the side effects has taken something, a part of me away. Maybe there is another medication or something that would counteract the side effects. Right now, my doctor is more interested in keeping me mentally well. I guess that is her job. Anyway, I am still hoping one day to feel normal again. Right now, I do not feel like being in any relationships. It causes a lot of unhappiness for me, but right now it is just another something for me to deal with.

## 02 July 1997

I have good news. At lease I have hope. I am not going to say the word yet, but I have tried an herbal mood enhancer; this being the second day and I actually feel good about myself. My mood has slowly progressed today in a positive manner. I don't feel hopeless or scared. I do not feel as they call it passively suicidal. It appears as though the "demons" have left me. If nothing else I am having a very good day. Have I stumbled upon something that is working? Working better than the conventional anti-depressants? Only time will tell.

## 16 July 1997

Yesterday was a good day. It was raining however so I took my clothes off the line outside and went to the laundromat. I was in a good mood, very peaceful. I was however, lacking energy. I was very tired. I finished my laundry and went home. I had a baked potato for lunch and set out to visit a friend of mine whom I had not seen in months. I visited for a couple of hours and she being a hair stylist cut my hair. A little later I left for home. Instead of going home I went to get a coffee and bumped into another friend. I then resumed my journey to a local department store and bought some pomade for my hair. Still exhausted, but in a good mood, I returned home.

I had supper and then decided to try to take a nap. Sleep never came and my friend Kevin called and wanted to come over for a visit. I suggested we go to get a coffee and he accepted this proposal. We sat around and talked. I felt as though I was going to fall asleep the whole time. If only I wasn't so tired.

Today I woke up and was in a depressed-like mood. For some reason I didn't wake up when I had to go to the bathroom and had an accident. I am still exhausted. I did wake up at least twice last night and made it downstairs.

I feel alone. I feel in ways useless and my self-esteem is very low. I really don't know where the day is going to take me. I am hoping that if what goes up comes down, then what goes down comes up. I talked to my sister today and all is well on the Pacific Coast.

I have decided that today I feel dirty. Not a sexual dirty, but rather a pumped full of drugs kind of dirty. This in addition to the uncomfortable depression-like feeling is making today a bit difficult. Rough night.

## 17 July 1997

Good morning. If how I wake up is any indication of how the day, today shall be a good day.

## 23 July 1997

Right now I am quite overwhelmed by life in general. I had a medication increase yesterday and I have felt bloated all day. Since I was trying a different brand of the herbal-antidepressant, I have been taking two tablets instead of three. I don't know if it has anything to do with today's depression. I don't want to do anything right now. I did some cleaning for my mother. Nothing fills this void. I tried calling my sister in California today, but there was no answer. I will keep trying. I feel so useless. Sometimes things that bring pleasure at times only makes things worse when I am in this state of mind. I am very lonely but I don't want to visit my friends. Actually, I don't want to leave the house at all. I am feeling afraid of things today. I called my case manager and told her how I was feeling. She said I had to keep trying to find something to do that would work. This meaning, to keep trying to find things that would occupy my thoughts. Be in control of the situation; don't let the situation be in control of you.

Right now I feel as if I had cried hysterically, then stopped. Life – I want so badly to have a normal life. I have not forgotten that I have

...And So Am I

the good days as well as some not so good days. The days have been getting harder. I am at present hoping not to become afraid of everything. I am functioning somewhat today. These things can build and build and then slowly take over. I can only pray. Even this seems to be in vain these days. I don't feel like someone is helping me. My philosophy on this is that since I am better than I was a few months ago, the being that sent me energy is letting me walk on my own two feet. I do miss the warmth and comfort very much. I don't know if it was a person, or other being but the presence is largely missed. It would make me feel better between freak bouts. I guess the best I can do now is to remember the special help I received and appreciate it. It is my guess that the help will come again if I ever need it.

### 24 July 1997

I have fought the side effects and symptoms for three days. Now they have subsided and I am tired now, but I am at peace mentally. At times I wish I would feel like this more regularly. Actually, I have been feeling better lately. The last few days have been a set back but I must have faith that things will improve. I am not as scared today which alone is an improvement over yesterday.

### 28 July 1997

There is so much to experience in this life. This is something that has been on my mind. I am afraid of experiencing things. I want very badly to get into acting. I am greatly inspired by other's work. I am afraid of the limitations I may not be able to overcome.

### 30 July 1997

Today I am going to a live concert. I am in good spirits despite medication side effects that tend to bring me down.

Last night I suddenly became tired (which is not abnormal) and I went to lie down. While I was lying there, I felt a presence. Subtle at first, then becoming a little stronger. I felt a combination of energies and a chill go down my right side of my body.

As I have mentioned before I am not good at listening but I remember hearing what sounded like a male voice. I do keep in mind that I am schizophrenic but this was a "good" voice. I really don't remember the conversation but I do remember the voice telling me that things should get a little better and that Jesus forgives me. I know what I felt, that was concrete to me. As for the voice of the messenger, I am unclear. I do not know who this presence was. Was it an angel or spirit? A person? This is unclear to me. All I know is that they didn't leave me after all. I will not feel as alone for a while.

### 19 Aug. 1997

The last few days have been rough going. The herbal anti-depressant does work, but I guess that in my case it is not effective enough. I am awaiting a call from my doctor in the hope of trying yet another anti-depressant. This will hopefully give me an edge and help me and help me cope with life. I love my life. Sometimes, though, I want to start over. This is why I am hoping the new medication will work with as few side effects as possible. There is so much I want to write down but at the same time, I don't want to allow this writing to become unnecessarily negative. I am not a negative person, but there are many negative forces acting upon my life right now.

Last night I went to a healing service. At the service there was a lot of praying and singing. We listened to a few people who actually had proof of healing; disappearing tumors, cancer, hearts healing. I hoped for the best. I figured it couldn't hurt, might help. People were falling to the floor as they were blessed. I didn't fall. I don't think that I was healed, but I guess the priest said, "God heals us all in different ways." I guess that it wasn't meant for me to be healed yet, mentally. I still believe that our hardships in this life are for a reason. I guess I wish that it was a little more tolerable. Sometimes it is difficult to keep my chin up. At times, all the encouragement in the world does little to help. At

...And So Am I

least, at the time. When times are good, life seems like something to be tackled. All things seem possible when things are going well. I love a challenge though, so I guess that is why I was chosen or chose to become ill. I guess it all depends on your perspective.

I haven't been hearing voices and the stress has been tolerable. Different parts of my body would shake (a nervous type shake) but I have learned to relax a bit and I have actually gained control over the shaking. This is something that I wondered if I could do, and I did it. I do catch myself occasionally, but I let go of the tension and it has been stopping.

### 27 Aug. 1997

Okay, I'm okay. The doctor I have at present put me on an anti-depressant. This is the second day on the new medication and so far, so good. No major side effects. I have been a bit fidgety, but it is a good change from the lethargic self I had become. As noted by my previous writing, the outcome is uncertain and unknown. I do have a good feeling about this one, though.

I have been going to the gym and hoping to get a good-looking body. I am not narcissistic, but I would like to turn my body fat into muscle. We'll see how persistent I am. Am I patient enough? I don't know. I got a friend to join the gym to motivate me. Again, we'll see.

### 28 Aug. 1997

Last night I felt a sense of peace for a few moments. It is relatively rare but encompasses my whole being. I wish I knew how to feel like that on my own at any given moment. The feeling is that of total well-being. I hope this will begin a new trend of peace. I can hope.

Today's journey has left me reading thoughts of wisdom. I am going to try to learn from it. Intentions don't get anything accomplished. I will try my best to do more now that I am feeling better and out of my rut. The gym has been proving to be beneficial. Along with the medication, it is giving me fulfillment. I still have a way to go before

I reach my goals, but taken one step at a time I might be able to make it up the mountain.

## 04 Sept. 1997

I am not sure if it is the new medication or the exercise but I have been feeling somewhat better lately. Today I am working on accepting and liking myself for who I am. It is not easy, but I think that with time I can raise my self-esteem to a decent level. I have to understand that I am doing well for a mentally ill person. I haven't given up. I have come close though. I've been working out and I was hoping to lose weight then gain it back as muscle. I guess it's too soon to expect any real results. I just need to be patient. It is all I can do.

Today, I am in relatively good spirits, but my physical energy level is low. I had a slow day at the gym. I didn't push myself as I had been. I will take one day at a time; little steps up the mountain path.

## 19 Oct. 1997

Well, it's been a little while since I've written. Quite a bit has been going on lately. I have gained a few inches on my waist probably in part due to the medications. My new psychiatrist told me to be careful because I could gain up to forty pounds on the medication prescribed to me for manic depression symptoms. My new doctor seems very nice. I told him I was still hoping for a miracle drug.

I haven't been going to the gym until this week after I tried on my pants and they didn't fit. I've gone twice this week and I am hoping to go today.

Also, on the topic of education, I may be on my way to being an English teacher. The woman at the department of education accepted my proposal to going to college to major in the English field. I tentatively will be starting in January. I am a little bit scared that I won't do well. Not that I think I am stupid, but I'm just concerned that my illness might get in the way. I guess all I can do is my best. Who knows, maybe I will even surprise myself. After all, it is only one class I will be starting out with this semester.

# Evolution

**18 Nov. 1997**

Recently, actually a few days ago, my doctor changed one of my medications. Today, I feel great. I feel (although it's a tricky word) normal. Tired, but normal. I am looking forward to today. I have been relatively happy all day and although I am being cautious, I haven't crashed. I am still having side effects, but I am getting used to them as much as I possibly can. The digestive problem is annoying to say the least, but it is usually a one-time deal. Then the rest of the day I am fine. My hair still falls out, but I guess it is the price I am paying for a shot at life. I know that I have had good days before, but today is different. If this is any indication of my future, then I must thank God. I feel like I can memorize; my mind is clear. I now feel there is going to be a future for me. Up until now, I did everything out of routine. I am enjoying writing this right now. I'm not ecstatic, but I am pleased to be able to write something positive. I feel alive for the first time in years.

Yesterday I did something I have not been able to do, to the best of my recollection, since I have been sick. I took a nap. No medications just on my own. I have been a little groggy with the new medication, but I actually fell asleep. In the recent past if I was tired, I would lie down and close my eyes, but wouldn't actually sleep; it was more of a meditation.

Maybe they finally found the right combination of drugs. It will take a little while before we know the outcome.

**19 Nov. 1997**

Last night I was a bit dizzy, which is a common side effect of the new medication, which should go away in a few days or so. I still feel pretty good. I guess you could say I am still adjusting, feeling this medication out. So far, so good. I feel full of life again. Somehow the illness made me feel much older than I am. Laughing was difficult and didn't feel good. At least not as good as it should have felt.

Socializing was a chore for me. I did so but it was very mechanical, very strained. I listened more than I spoke. I have noticed a change in the manner others approach me, and lately they have even been speaking to me. I pray that this relief I am feeling stays for a while. Life seems more worthwhile. My faults and shortcomings are not prominently staring me in the face. I am feeling a sense of freedom I have not felt in years. Yes, maybe we are getting somewhere.

Today I am again in a good frame of mind. I woke up early this morning and was groggy at first, but after my coffee and a couple of cigarettes, I was feeling pretty good. I am like an infant learning something new. This enthusiasm of life is great, but it will need some getting used to. I hope that I won't lose it.

My mood has been stable. My stress has been under control. I have not heard any voices lately and I am not depressed. It has been a few days now that I have felt good, so I will assume these changes are going to stay for a while. I say this because sometimes when you take a new medication you feel elated for a day or two and then your body adjusts and you're back down again. It has been about a week now that I have been taking this drug and I still feel well.

I took a moment and called my health clinic and thanked them. The receptionist whom I adore – she's a sweetheart – said she would pass the word that I was feeling better along. She said she doesn't get many positive calls. That is part of the reason why I called. I felt it was appropriate even if it had only been two good days in a row. I am still happy, possibly content or at peace. It is difficult to describe how I feel.

I went to work today because the theatre was running low on popcorn. Popping corn is my least favorite job, but for the most part I was pretty much in a relatively good mood. I caught myself getting a bit low, so I tried to focus on getting back up. At first I thought that I was going to crash hard, but it didn't happen. Faith. I guess it was the old feeling of being overwhelmed; it was a bit scary. I don't want to make any false hope for this new drug, but I have been feeling pretty good the last few days. I have been a bit shaky (tremors) and have caught myself slurring words; not noticeably to others. (At least no one has commented on it.)

Things aren't bothering me as they used to. I think that is part of the reason I am feeling so good. I am not at a euphoric state, but this peace is very much welcomed. I feel like doing things. I feel relatively good about myself.

### 20 Nov. 1997

I woke up early this morning to the commotion of my brother and sister getting ready for school. Although I have been woken up early before this new medication, I have been doing so more frequently the last few days. I am dreaming at night, although I don't recollect what they were about. This is relatively new because before I didn't dream if that is possible or I just wouldn't remember them for the most part.

When I woke up this morning I was a bit disoriented which as I mentioned before is not a new feeling. I was just like, "Oh, no. I hope I am not back to this again." About an hour later I was back to my new self, a little shaky today, still. I feel a little bit spacey but feel as if I can remember things. I guess my mind is clearer.

I think that anyone who has a chronic illness or condition is totally grateful when they find something to control the symptoms (a cure is not necessarily a possibility) at least I would imagine so. I think a few pages back I mentioned a healing service. People were on a religious high (which is not necessarily a bad thing in itself) and were eager and ecstatic to reveal their spiritual or physical healings. I am not discrediting anything. We must be patient. I can't stress this enough. I must learn to be patient with myself, first.

When you are sick, you must keep your FIGHT at whatever the cost. I know that up until recently especially before the new medication I had lost most of my fight and was on auto-pilot just trying to make it through days that were very long. I got my fight back about two weeks ago. It just happened. My definition of "fight" is the will to overcome something that is very difficult for you. In this case it refers to the strength; an inner strength which helps one's journey through life conquering hardships. I have also learned but seldom used anger as a means of achieving goals. Anger can be directed positively. It can give you the fight if it is not changed into hostility. It is a normal emotion, which should be expressed (although I am guilty of suppressing it) and then released if possible.

Okay, I feel good. I am waiting to crash. After about three years of conditioning I have not let go and let myself be happy. I worked at being mundane. This is the fourth day I have been up and haven't really crashed. I have had other emotions besides being up. I have been bored and have had traces of unhappiness and fear. I also had the beginning of a panic attack but I have been trying to work through the stress without taking extra medications.

Although I try to be the best man I possibly can be I have my own faults and vices. For me, nicotine and caffeine make me a junkie. I am on four different medications now which I am not supposed to drink alcohol with. I have been told that my symptoms may increase with this or other substances. Once in a while I pay the price. I never was a heavy drinker nor do I intend to become one. A six-pack lasts me at least two days. I am not going to say that it is an intelligent move but once in a while even schizoaffective people may like to have a beer or two if they are of age. This is not an endorsement of mixing medications with alcohol. If alcohol is not for you, I respect the fact. I suppose that for me in the past, alcohol was an escape. I must now learn to savor my sobriety. It is a gift in itself.

For the record, I live in a house where no one has ever smoked a cigarette (except for me) and alcohol is basically taboo. I might finish a six pack in two or more days. My father will finish off a six pack in about a year. No kidding. I just wanted to state that I thought that it is amazing, that's all. If I drink, it is maybe once or twice a month. In a way, I do it so I know what to expect. If you're in a social situation and you happen to forget (as simple as it sounds), you don't want to find out too late what might happen. I want to know how much control I will have after, say, a beer. This is my personal opinion, which is not intended to encourage usage. Like I said, I think that people who don't drink or smoke are amazing.

I am now faced with a decision. Should I resume my work as a volunteer at the nursing home? I feel great, but my hands are very shaky. It will be difficult to paint the nails while shaking. I suppose I could do it, but it will be hard. I love the people there. They are great. I stopped going a few months back because it had become a mental chore. I was getting little satisfaction from my act of volunteering itself. This is in my opinion when you need to take a step back and admit that you need a break. Volunteering is something that should come from the heart.

I feel free. I feel less dependent. I hope I never take this for granted. Even if I was to get sick again tomorrow, it will have been a great few days. It has been about four years since I have felt like this. I still have my share of side effects to contend with, but right now I would say it was worth it. I guess you must know pain to know pleasure.

I love to write. Will I become an English teacher? I don't know. I am really excited. I feel pretty confident about myself. The whole world seems changed to me somehow. I really want to be a film actor. My sister is plugging away at her acting career in California still. Maybe if she makes it she can help me in the door. I feel as though I can memorize more now. My mind is less cloudy. I hope that it is not just an illusion. This time I don't think it is. My writing has picked up and is headed in a positive direction. Where there was hopelessness there is now a little ray of hope.

It is difficult to live with no hope, insecurity and dependence on others; feeling blindly in the dark trying to find a purpose. I think those days are over now. I could still have bad days (not that everyone doesn't) but I have faith they won't stay for long. Live in the present; I have to remind myself. The past wounds have scarred over. The future comes as it must in due time. To some degree you need to work on the future through planning, but it is useless to worry about possible outcomes.

I have been keeping busy with my reading and watching movies. I have been keeping my medical appointments and still have my job at the movie theatre on weekends. I don't get bored. Today is Thursday. Every Thursday I go get my paycheck and go grocery shopping. I have stuck with fruit juices in the place of soda. I buy yogurt and fruit for breakfast, macaroni and/or burritos for lunch and I have a can of tuna for supper. I buy extra fruit for snacks. On occasion I eat with the family. One might suppose that on this diet I would be losing weight. On the contrary, I have actually been gaining weight. I have made the assumption that it is probably the side effect of one of two medicines I take, which could have this effect.

I really want to go to the gym, but I am taking it easy because of the new medication. I am not making excuses, but I want to know how this new med is going to affect me. On the cautions it said that exercise could cause dizziness. It also said listed on the possible effects as constipation. The reason I bring this up is that another med causes me to have diarrhea. My personal joke is that maybe they will cancel each other out and things will go back to regular. Wouldn't that be something?

I called Dawn and told her how well I was feeling. She said that it was great. She said she would call me back after 3:30. I have to pick up my sister at the school and bring her to work. I told Dawn that she could now meet the real me.

**21 Nov. 1997**

It is now a few minutes past midnight. Tonight I visited my friend Sarah Elizabeth and we went to her mother's house for supper. I was bubbling with energy for a while. Although we have been friends for a while, I (jokingly) introduced myself. The reason got the last gesture was understood after I explained I was in my opinion, the real me. Sarah's mother has MPD and is very understanding. She is quite frankly one of the nicest people I have ever met.

It has only been a few days now since I have mostly felt like myself but I can already see some of the reason why I went through what I did. Since my illness, I have become friends with wonderful people who have different ills of their own. In reality (not that everyone doesn't have their own fights) now my closest friends have battles that they are waging. I guess we are here to help one another through the good and the bad. I am almost twenty-six years old now and most of my friends I had before I got sick have drifted away. Was it my illness? Did I unconsciously withdraw myself? All I know is this: True friends stick together.

There is a girl whom I love very much. Her name is Courtney and she and I have been friends since preschool; if you can believe it. She has been there for me over the years. The cross that she gave me when I was in the hospital is still around my neck. I can't think of anything that would make me take it off. It is a reminder, of the past and the present. I consider it to be a symbol of love since it was given to me out of love. It is a representation also of the cross I must bear myself. Now Court and I are still very close, but we have drifted a bit. I work mostly weekends and she works weekdays. She spends most of her free time with her present beau. Last time I saw her she said that we would go for a coffee sometime. This is good enough for me. I love her as much as anyone can love someone.

...And So Am I

I still feel good. Earlier tonight I started to get a bit low but it was only temporary. I think we are beginning to get somewhere. By we, I mean everyone who has helped me through this. The doctor, my counselor, my case manager and even the receptionist has played a part in the success I have recently encountered. The doctors' monitor the medications and checks and balances it. The counselor is there for support in the everyday troubles faced. The case manager, who I couldn't live without, does a slew of things from objective counseling and helping me with some very tedious paperwork and forms. Then there is the receptionist. She has helped me in many ways over the last few years; directing calls and just being there like a friend. I remember an instance when I was very agitated and couldn't sit still. She periodically would open the window and talk to me. This calmed me down. She treated me like a person; not a freak. I have great respect for all these people. I must take a moment to thank anyone I have forgotten. Thanks.

It is about 7:30am and I feel all right. Although I do not consider myself a morning person, I don't feel the usual grogginess that comes with mornings. I feel ready to face the day. I hope that I can get myself to the gym before I have to work tonight.

I had the strangest dream last night. I have been dreaming more often now. I dreamed that I had the name of my new medication tattooed on my butt. I had been jokingly telling people, my friends and family that I was going to do just that if the medication worked. Not that I really would but I thought you might get a kick out of that.

Okay, it has taken me about three days but I now understand some new feelings I am experiencing. These words only partially describe how I feel. I feel equal to my peers. This is something that I haven't felt since my illness began. I feel worthy to experience life. I have been. I am even noticing that I am enjoying memories of things that I wasn't able to enjoy. An example of this is a movie I had watched a few months ago. I thought it was a good film, but I was stifled as far as enjoyment. I caught myself thinking, "Wow, that was a good movie," and I felt good about feeling good about it. (That was a little redundant.) It is like I have been asleep through the last few years. I read a book about this topic, about how people sleep through life and only when they are awake can they fully enjoy life. In my case, I had been sleepwalking through life because of my illness and the side effects of the medications. I had tried very hard to wake up and I had some improvement, but it is nothing compared to how alive I feel now. It seems to be the right combination of meds. I pray I never take this new gift for granted and go back to sleep.

## 22 Nov. 1997

Last night I was a little low while I was at work. My suspicion for this is that I got up really early and I drank about two pots of coffee. I really need to invest in some decaf, don't you think? Anyway, the low came after the coffee. I was still in a better mood than before this new med.

I had the courage last night to ask a girl I work with on a date. No set date. She said yes.

Aside from all the new positive changes I have made a discovery that might alter my habits a bit. Before this new medicine I would drink a pot of coffee and it wouldn't phase me. I could chain smoke four or five cigarettes in a row. Now, I have been noticing that I am a bit tired when I first get up. Then I am full of energy. Although the medications are working great, I have been noticing that caffeine and nicotine now affect my mood. I have had excessive caffeine and discovered that my energy level fell. I guess this is a normal reaction, but it is one that is new to me. I guess that I, along with the majority of the people of the world want to be as happy as possible. The happier the better, right? I am at peace mentally and am grateful to everyone who has helped me achieve this level.

Something else has evolved since the new medicine. I used to feel stupid; my memory was poor and I got confused easily. I didn't learn fast. An example was the job at the video store. Has my intelli-

...And So Am I

gence been increased? I guess I just need to say that I don't feel stupid anymore.

## 23 Nov. 1997

It is one in the morning and I just got back from visiting Sarah. Although she can't see it, I see her progress. She is becoming more self-confident. She seems to be enjoying her schooling where she has a class taking care of young children.

It has been snowing all day and the roads were partly cleared. I took my time coming home.

Today I woke up early and got ready for work. I arrived at work early, and the manager sent me to the bank for a coin order. I was lucky and got to tear tickets, which is my favorite job. As with life in general, this job can be done in several ways. Some people just tear the tickets. I try to be more personable. I say, "Hello" and thank the customer. I also compliment customers if they have nice nails or a cool shirt, etc. I got my review and got one of the highest scores for customer service. I think he said I had the highest. When I talk to the customers, I let it come from the heart. I am sincere (most of the time) while in customer contact. Then I was asked if I would stay an extra three hours and pop popcorn. I agreed and popped about ten trash bags full of corn. It is my least favorite task, but I get to listen to music so it isn't that bad.

The people whom I work with have noticed a change in my over all actions and appearance for the better. I have noticed that some of my coworkers are actually talking to me know. I don't think the anti-social behavior was specifically from them or myself, but I have noticed a change. I think it is really neat.

I have been slurring my words, which could be a side effect of two of my meds. I am going to work at it. It is something that bothers me so I am going to change it.

I feel well, so am I? This is something that any ill person deals with. I do however have to take four different medications to achieve this state of being. One of the biggest reasons for re-hospitalization is that the patient feels well and stops taking their medication. I am hopefully, after all the changes, able to realize the importance of the medications. I take my medications regularly in the morning when I get up, and about an hour before bedtime. I don't like having to swallow pills twice a day, but I would like to stay healthy. They are now a part of my life. It's not that bad.

**24 Nov. 1997**

Today I am beginning to get used to the new med. I was a little less euphoric and more down to earth. I know that I am feeling better because I actually felt anger today. I was at the gym riding the exercise bike watching television. I was the only one up there, so I turned off the other TV and put the one in front of me on a music station. About twenty minutes later a woman got on the bike next to me. A third man came up and put on the other TV and turned off the television I was watching. I realize that I should have said something at that time, it then might not have been such an annoyance.

I was on a quest last night. I wanted to know a little more than the pharmacy precaution list about this new drug. There was nothing about it in my mother's book on medications. This was not a surprise. I began an adventure to the bookstore. I looked through book after book, searching for something. If it is on the market there must be something on it, right? When I thought that I had looked through all of the books, I found in a corner, a stack of 1998 nurses pill guides. I was not about to pay $30 – for less than a page, some of which I already knew. I did learn something about this drug though. It said that something about how alcohol dilutes the drug via the liver. Therefore, alcohol is probably not a good idea. Another thing that it said, which surprised me, was that nicotine also has a diluting effect on the drug. Wow, huh…

Right now I am sitting in a local coffee shop sipping coffee. I must tell you that I am putting an effort towards my health. I got half decaf and half regular. Much to my dismay, it is to my palate, terrible. I guess I am not used to it. I drink my coffee black and this mix is very bitter.

I don't know if I am ready for a relationship right now or not. I kind of wanted a break for a little while. After the bookstore, I went to the movie theatre where I work and a girl, who I really like, was there. I surprised her with a rose. She was happy, but I don't have the slightest clue what she was thinking. Until recently, I considered my "personality" to be how can I put it delicately, boring. I just didn't know what to say. I would like to establish a friendship with her so we could get to know each other. Maybe she is not the one for me. She has a pretty face with short, wavy hair. But, what I like most about her is her personality and her mind. I asked her earlier if she'd go for a coffee with me and she said yes, but she didn't like coffee. I guess it is a start.

The movie I went to see was good…not great, but well done. The make-up and wigs used to change one of the characters' identity was amazing.

I am finding that I am smoking a little less today. I haven't felt bad at all today except for a mild but persistent headache from the anti-depressant.

On my way to the gym I stopped to go to the bathroom at one of my favorite stores. Since my weight gain most of my pants are between tight and way too tight. Anyway, to make a long story short, I found a pair of jeans in my size of my favorite brand. I put them back and went to go to my car. I lit a cigarette and walked down the sidewalk a bit and then turned around. This being a discount brand name store, the items seldom last for very long on the shelf. I decided that $25.00 wasn't bad for a pair of pants that fit so I caved in and got out the plastic.

I called my sister in California and talked to her briefly while she put on her make-up to go out. She had an audition for a commercial. One of her agents saw a picture of me and said I had a good look.

I reached Izzy-mom, a friend of mine, whom I happened to find her number after quite some time. She moved to Ohio with her husband and two children about the time I was beginning to get sick. I was for the most part well, when we were close. She was happy I was doing well.

I also called a priest-friend of mine. He was happy that I was getting better and asked me to call him next Monday for directions to his church. It will be nice to see him.

I feel as though I am healing.

I got a raise today from the theatre. I am not sure how much it will be, but the largest raises given are a quarter.

I was able to take a nap on my own today.

## 25 Nov. 1997

My mind is clear and it is taking less effort to memorize things. I don't feel like I am always forgetting something. I am still at peace with myself. I haven't taken any PRN's for stress lately.

I am finding the world to be a different place. If things keep going as they are I feel confident that things are going to work out. This is an outlook that would not have been possible just a few weeks ago. It is not that I didn't try, but everything is so much easier when you are feeling well. I hope that this health continues, but even if it doesn't it will have been worth it.

I have to watch my eating habits. Today, I had a yogurt and a pear and then went to the gym. I prefer to go after lunch but I had to pick up my sister at school so I opted to go earlier. Then I basically forgot to eat until about 2:30 when I began to feel weak and then had some tuna and two bowls of cereal. It became a binge. I need to make my eating more regular, but I've never been very good at that.

I know that I am feeling better because I am beginning to floss more regularly. Before I got sick, I would floss my teeth once or twice a day. When I became ill, it was one of the last things on my mind to do. It is not to say that personal hygiene wasn't done, it was however, because of low self-esteem quite the chore. Right now I look forward to shaving, showering and dental care.

I had long hair in the back and was growing it out when I got sick. When the symptoms got bad I cut it all off and shaved the back. Although there have been days when I felt like getting my head shaved, I have been trying to grow out my hair. It is all one length now, dirty blond, and it comes down to the bottom of my chin. My hair grows slowly compared to most people I know. Last winter I had my hair dyed brown. It was really neat for about a week and then began to wash out. As it was washing out, my hair seemed dirty to me. Would I do it again? Possibly. Would I bleach it? It is less likely, but it is possible. After all, I love acting. I have had a lot of practice over the past few years. I had to try to act as if I were well. I really did. I used techniques that I learned when I was eleven years old at a local children's theatre. We would say, "Oh, a tie" and say it in different ways. Examples of this would be ecstatic, bored, disinterested, and the like.

At work I would do my best to make, "Good 'n' you" sound honest and sincere. I would have to act upbeat when greeting customers. I have had only a couple of instances where a customer said things like, "Things can't be that bad." I think that was pretty good for a three year period of time. I wanted to scream at him, "If you only knew!" but I had to resort to, "Thank you, enjoy the show."

I am looking forward to going back to school. I really am. I was supposed to meet with the vocational rehabilitation counselor tomorrow – she left a message to reschedule. The process of actually getting to school is not going to be an easy one. I have a feeling that it is going to be a last minute rush but, there I go bringing the future into the present again.

## 28 Nov. 1997

I am sipping a hot chocolate and trying to relax. The last couple of days have been noteworthy. Wednesday I went to the gym and kept the RPM's up. I pushed myself a little harder than usual but it felt good.

I then went to work. I thought that I might get away with not popping corn, but I got called upon to do so. I popped ten trash bags full of corn in four hours. I was relatively content with the music playing.

I got a decent paycheck this week and I will not need to use my credit card to buy food this week.

I woke up early Thanksgiving morning with the intention of going to the gym, but I opted to stick around in case anyone needed help. I did some cleaning. It was a slow day. Then we all ate. We gave thanks for things in the past year and I thanked everyone for their help in my achieving the state I am in.

It is far from perfect, I had yet to learn. It may be normal emotions that I haven't experienced in a while. Anyway, after Thanksgiving dinner, I went for a drive to the movie theatre to try and cheer up a friend of mine who got stuck working. I brought her a lemon-aid. I was not expecting any big reaction but I left feeling low. All day I was fighting an intense desire to rock and pace. I was getting a bit frustrated that the new medicine was perhaps like the rest. A couple days of peace and then back to the frustrated self I go. My mood did improve however, and so there is still hope. I wish it could stay like the first week, but I guess I have to be accepting and realistic.

Despite all the warnings, I considered buying a six-pack. I fought the urges and tried working on relaxing and breathing. I even opted to take stress medication but didn't. After about an hour I began to feel better. I guess I will have to learn the new emotions and learn how to deal with them.

I have been staying up later and getting up earlier. It's something. I used to try to sleep all day if I could to escape my mind. I guess today was a low day. If the patterns of the past still hold true, about one good week then one bad week, I can learn to deal with it. It still wasn't that bad. I was depressed a bit, which is usually hard to get out of. I still have some FIGHT left in me.

...And So Am I

I talked to my sister about everything and nothing at all. It was great to hear from her. I miss her. She might come home for a week in January.

I guess all the medications have their limitations for what they accomplish or control. I was just hoping for a miracle. I guess I'm okay. I wish I could say I am good but I will save that for tomorrow. The chocolate is delicious.

## 30 Nov. 1997

The last two days I worked. Nothing really notable about work. I did notice that I was happy and slowly got tired as the shift progressed a little more so than usual, but not too bad. After work, although I was tired, I went up to see a video at Sarah's.

People have been commenting on my appearance. It seem to show that I am feeling better. I am working on the pacing. I am having a hard time standing still. I can sit still but standing is difficult. I am slowly working on it. It was there to some degree since I first began to get sick. I am more relaxed, but I still fidget. All in all, today was a good day. A couple of days ago, although I was fighting it at first, I heard a voice say, "You are going to be okay." I don't listen or act upon the voices now, but hopefully this one, a "good" voice, will prove true.

I love my new life. I am hoping to help others on their way. I don't have answers to other people's problems, and I don't pretend to. I can think a little better now and may be able to help a little, sometimes doing nothing at all is the best solution. An example of this was when someone I knew was "bummed out." I said to myself not to let it become my problem (as I sometimes do). I think that this is a healthy approach. I gave my support but didn't absorb the negativity. In any case any advice given is that which I remembered from self-help literature I have read or skills that have been instilled in me otherwise. I am not going to give in to the victim/CO-dependent roles some relationships tend to encourage. I've been there, I didn't like it then and I am not about to take it again. I have learned that people are there to help you when you need them, but you need to be the one to work towards what you view that health consists of. I believe that for the most part, I am getting closer to health. At this given moment, I feel healthy but I know that even healthy people have good and bad moments, good and bad days. I have already experienced this fluctuation, which was in reality normal. Ideally, I would love to be happy all the time, but who wouldn't. It is not realistic. Without pain, you cannot experience pleasure; or so I've been told or read somewhere.

I have been feeling like me. It has been an awkward transition, but a rather quick one; at least if you consider how long it took before I was treated, and how long I felt sick. It was about four years since I have felt this good. Sometimes I feel like I have a mild hangover and my body and joints seem to be swelling. This is from the new med. It doesn't really bother me much. I take a pain reliever, which takes care of the hangover quite well, but my joints are still a bit sore. It is still a small price to pay for the relief that I have been given. I think that even if it doesn't last, the peace will have made it worth it. I am not intending to be pessimistic.

With any luck I will be able to learn how to be still. I can stand still if I am leaning against something, but for on my own I rock back and forth. I am starting the process of using will power to slow it down, which is actually working. I now need to learn to stop it. I know it sounds a bit odd, but one of the reasons I pace is because it feels good. I don't know why. Maybe it is something like an exercise high or some sort of release of endorphins or the like.

I took my nighttime medications and am starting to get sleepy. I love writing and all the pleasures that had been a void only two weeks ago. Food tastes really good. Breathing is relaxing. I can't wait to go back to the gym. Exercise is a good high. I like my job and the people; except popping corn. I have been more social and have been calling people.

I have to get up early tomorrow so I will leave off here for now. Peace.

I woke up quite early this morning and enjoyed the sunrise with a cup of coffee. It is now eleven o'clock and I am in a very good mood. I went to the gym this morning and worked out on the bike for about forty minutes. Usually I try for a bit longer but the coffee wanted out.

## 02 Dec. 1997

Today as with lately, I have been getting up relatively early, for me. I got up around seven and felt good; well rested. I then did my daily morning routine. (I am still flossing, by the way). I met with my case manager at eleven. I told her how much better I have been feeling and she was pleased. I told her that the exercises to find good things in life would be much easier now, and that I feel confident about school. I told her about the voices I heard.

The pacing is beginning to slow down a little. I can now stand still if I will myself to. I bought a video today and later watched it with Sarah. It came with a small sticker with the lead actor on it. You are supposed to collect the stickers, like this one, from this movie company to get a discount on a future purchase. I opted to put the sticker on my rearview mirror to replace another sticker, which I had coincidentally removed today because I had grown tired of it. The sticker placed on my rearview mirror is my personal reminder of Sam. I don't need the sticker to remember him, but it was a promise that I made to myself when I got out of the hospital.

I have been feeling a bit of anger recently. It is not necessarily a bad thing. I wish I could perpetually be happy, but it is not realistic. Today I am angry because I have to pick my sister up after school. Then I have to pick my brother up after his drama club practice. I then have to bring my sister to work and then pick her up after work. I am angry because this is the third week or so and I asked them to find a ride for tomorrow. (They could take the bus). I wanted to have tomorrow for myself so that I could do my monthly errands. I am angry because I work every weekend. I just wanted a day where I don't have to do anything if I wish not to do so. It is catching up with me. I just want a day here and there. I don't feel it is too much to ask for. It is Tuesday and it looks like the first day off is going to be this Sunday. For the record, I don't want to appear to be cold hearted. I usually don't mind picking up the siblings. It is however starting to become somewhat on the unappreciative side. I am respecting of others' feelings, but I also need to tend to my own.

## 04 Dec. 1997

Today, I was woken up by my mother hollering. My sister and brother are both immune to the sound of their alarm clocks. I used to sleep through the morning routine but since I have been feeling better, I have been getting up earlier. I got ready and set out to register my car.

Upon arriving home I was in a good mood. Yesterday someone tried to talk to me in my mind, but I couldn't hear. I could however feel. It was similar to the previous energies feel, but seemed more persistent. I thought it might have been Sam, but I am not sure that there has been any contact since the early stages of my illness. Although the medications stop the hallucinations, they also make it much more difficult to hear the "good" voices when they try to speak to me. It was however a fair trade-off. I don't have all the answers. Sometimes I wish I did, other times I am glad I don't.

I have seen images in the clouds for years now, once in a while. It requires imagination. Is it only imagination? I honestly don't believe that, but this is one of those things I will leave up to you. At one point they were frequent, and I actually took photographs of them. One of my favorites was a symbol of a never ending world or at least my interpretation, which came at a low point, when I believed we were in our last days. I saw an angel in the clouds. It was images that were familiar to me. That was the past.

In the present, (which is now the past too), I was sitting on the porch and looking up at a cloud formation and thought to myself that I hadn't seen any pictures in the clouds for quite some time. I said a

...And So Am I

little prayer. It then began to form into the world without end symbol. I was put at ease with this. Then I saw an eye. The eye changed into a likeness of Jesus. The beard, mustache and something on his head that looked to me like a "crown of thorns," but could also have been merely a halo. This picture disturbed me because he seemed to look very sad. I had the belief that he was a happy God. As it sometimes does, as surely as the wind blows, the picture of Jesus began to change. The thorns turned into hair. The mouth changed along with the nose. I sat in shock as the image reflected that of my good friend Bea. I met her at the nursing home, and I used to do her nails before I decided that I was having a hard time helping. I met the nursing home activity director who told me that Bea missed me "terribly." I then later met up with the physical therapist and she also told me the same thing. I guess praying for her in this case was not enough.

The cloud formation made me stop procrastinating. I picked up a rose at a local floral shop and set out for the nursing home. I saw the activity director and she walked me to Bea's room. The door was closed but she knocked and said to Bea, "You got a special Christmas gift." She wheeled her to the hall and got me a chair. Bea was weeping. "I'm so happy." She told me that she was beginning to have trouble with her good hand and couldn't feed herself any longer. She was a little bit difficult to understand through the tears. I didn't know what to do. She cried the whole time I was there. I held her hand and I kissed her cheek. I told her about my plans for school. She asked me about my non-existent modeling career.

I just don't know how to feel about this experience. I told the management that I would try to return to following Monday to do her nails. I wish I could do more for her but I think that is my best. This is one of those times I wish I knew the right answer.

Today was a pretty good day, all in all. I realized how much I missed the people at the nursing home. Was it a message from God for me to get off my butt and do something with my life now that I was feeling good again?

We all have been given the gift of free will, but I believe He is there to give us a hand or a little nudge here and there. I may be wrong about the belief that the mental illness was a learning experience. I have become more tolerant to differences. I am still waking up. I feel as if I am focusing or adjusting. I am not quite in sync with the world just yet. I am slowly getting closer to it each day. I'm learning to accept, but not take for granted, the peace from within I feel. I wish everyone could feel the peace. I guess it comes in contrast to the years of depression and lethargy. I haven't been to the gym in a couple of days but I am hoping that along with my new energy I will get a little closer to my original size. My joints are still swollen, as they have been, but they are beginning to go down a little.

Tomorrow is my father's birthday. I am scheduled to work, so I don't know what they will do about the party. I don't know. I must bring myself back to the present.

## 11 Dec. 1997

A lot has transpired since my dad's birthday. I missed the party but he waited to open my gift.

Monday I called to get my credit balance and the automated machine said zero. I had just made a payment of four hundred dollars. I called to talk to a real person who told me I had a $524.24 purchase and an attempted $600 purchase. The woman on the phone gave me several phone numbers to call. The second woman asked me if I had my card in my possession. I told her yes. It was the number I read off to her. It didn't sink in until the next day that my second card, which I didn't use, was missing. (I had two credit cards on the same account.) I also made a conclusion that it had been stolen out of my gym locker. I grew up in a small town where locks on lockers were a rarity. I had been going to the gym for about two years - I never imagined this would happen.

Tuesday I cleaned out my bank account and bought a candle holder and three packs of cigarettes. Tuesday night I gave my brother one remaining pack and asked him to lock it up. This is something that I have done before. Wednesday I got out the nicotine gum and began chewing. I had five pieces of gum. I believe that this is the equivalent of one pack of cigarettes. I think for me that it is pretty good. Today however, I have decided to go cold turkey. It is five p.m. and I have not had a single cigarette. Today was honestly not much more difficult than with the gum. I decided that if I could not smoke because I didn't have the money, maybe it was for the best. I got paid today, but I bought food, gas, juice and coffee. About four o'clock I had an idea. I am not big on candy, although I have been munching mints like mad today. I bought a second toothbrush to play with. It seems to be working well. If I can make it through today I think I can do it. For the record though, I love smoking. I am an addict. I probably always will be. In all honesty, I have noticed that the nicotine patches or the gum actually made me have more nicotine fits.

This is the last page of the first notebook, thus being the ninetieth handwritten page. I am patiently awaiting copying the writing to computer format.

## 15 Dec. 1997

The job is really bothering me. I didn't work today, but the new corporate takeover has taken every last bit of individuality we had left. We have to suggest items and encourage them to purchase the larger sizes. We have to do random theatre checks. The word "Welcome" is driving me insane. Maybe it is time for a new job, I don't know. Where would I go? I guess I will do my best for now. I believe in trying to make the customer happy, but I don't believe in forcing someone to buy a four dollar popcorn just because it comes with a free refill. I got stuck popping both days this week. Why, I am not sure. I am not very happy with that. What can I do? I worked for the theatre for three years. Now it is a new beginning. No holiday party this year. With this new company, if we do everything correctly, we get a monetary bonus.

## 21 Dec. 1997

We all act. Some ad-lib but for the most part we are all playing roles for society. There are some sub-divisions among the societies. For example work. It is a sort of society, is it not? Among the workers there are people whose role is to govern them. This is generically known as the big-wigs or just the boss. The workers have their own society, which may or may not include the bosses.

The workers and bosses have families and friends; aren't those sub-divisions of sub-divisions? Does this make sense? In each sub-division of society we act in different manners.

## 22 Dec. 1997

Today I got up early and went to work. I tore tickets today and was in a good mood. I looked at the sky and saw beauty. It is very difficult to explain the feeling of peace and well being that I have had lately. I love my new life. It is presently about three in the morning and although I'm tired, I am relishing the sense of well-being. It is not a manic high, although the sense of peace is so strong that if I didn't know better it could be confused.

After work I browsed around a discount store for about an hour then headed home. I was exhausted and took a nap. Sarah called me about 7:30 pm and said they were having a little birthday party for her mom and invited me up. I told her I'd be there in about an hour. I went to a local grocery store to buy something for her. I picked out a delicately colored peach rose. I arrived at their house in about an hour and presented the rose. She loved it. Sarah brought out a cake.

After the party Sarah's mom presented me with a gift for me for Christmas. I unwrapped the box and lifted off the cover. Inside the box was a hand made Hopi hair clip. Being somewhat unconventional, I loved it and replaced the elastic with the bear-paw clip. Since they are hand-carved, they are usually quite expensive.

I talked with Sarah until one a.m. and then went to get a coffee. I chatted a bit with the server then went home.

...And So Am I

Tomorrow, (actually today) I am going to go to the nursing home to paint Bea's nails. I actually miss her and am looking forward to seeing her. It is a task that is rewarding. Right now I am looking forward to seeing her. It is a task that is rewarding. Right now I am only doing her nails, but it took me an hour and a half to do her nails last time. Surprisingly, the time actually goes by pretty quickly. I just have to be patient. This is a quality I hope I can improve upon in time.

Life gives us so many lessons. I must learn to let go of negative things. I am open to new things and am enjoying the good times.

## 23 Dec. 1997

It snowed a foot and a half today. I figured that God "is." I can't really explain but it is my new feeling on the subject.

Today I was a bit low, as I usually am when it snows for whatever reason, but I was blessed by the powers that be. As I said earlier, I was feeling low, so I lied down to sleep it off. Anyway, as I was relaxing I saw a vision of a candle much like the one I had burning. It was like seeing something with your eyes closed. It left me with a good feeling.

I have also realized that I have stopped pacing altogether; if you can believe it. I have also lost up to an inch off my waist.

## 28 Dec. 1997

I had a good birthday yesterday. I got a new comforter and other items, which may prove to come in handy. I felt so much love today.

I haven't been sleeping well lately and it has made me a bit moodier than normal. I am going to sleep in tomorrow, if I'm able to do so.

I have been seeing more colors but not enough to really prove useful in any way. I have noticed that I am sensitive to those around me. I seem to pick up on their emotions which is both awesome and frustrating at the same time. It has given me a better understanding of the actions of others. I actually feel at times what others feel. Could this explain some of my mania? Maybe not.

Right now I am exhausted from my birthday and work. I still feel at peace.

## 31 Dec. 1997

I got my hair trimmed yesterday. The stylist who is also a friend told me that the cut was "on the house." I used some of the money to buy supplies for the nursing home.

My medical insurance is a big mess right now. I am not "in" yet for this month due to human error. The pharmacy gave me some of my medications to get by on my word that I would soon be "in." The drugs I take cost about seven hundred dollars a month. I feel really bad that it is now the end of the month, I should have been "in" long before I was about to run out of medication. I am waiting now at the doctor's office waiting for a nurse to come in to get samples. I am in a relatively good mood. People have been telling me things like, "You are one of the happiest guys I've ever met," and, "Lay off the coffee." In any case I am pretty happy although I still get my bad moods just like everyone else.

I am not really seeing auras but I have been seeing "emotions" in my third eye with flashes of color here and there. I thank God for these glimpses of love and am trying to be patient. I don't think that I would be very healthy if everything happened all at once.

I am trying to keep everything in perspective and I believe all things happen for a reason. I am working on living in the present and letting go of the negatives of the past.

I seem to have made some sense of the taps that I have been feeling for the past four years. It is starting to tell me to relax that part of my body. Maybe I have an energy block or I am closing up. I am still not certain on this, but this is my new theory. Who it is, is another story, but I have been feeling a lot of energy, which to me is better than any drug. It is not to say that drugs theoretically cause similar effects. For the most part, with my new medications and my faith, I am happy with my life.

...And So Am I

## 27 Jan. 1998

I haven't written in a few weeks. I got bronchitis and was feeling low, but didn't go to see the doctor because my insurance wasn't "in" yet. To get "in" I have to incur medical bills with a particular amount. It is called a spend down. It is quite similar to a deductible. I actually have two "insurance" companies, but there are holes in both. It is not a simple process.

Around the 14th of the month, I was finally "in" and filled my prescriptions. This was a Saturday. On Monday I went to my primary care physician and she listened to my lungs and prescribed an anti-biotic, which I had taken at least a few times before. About two days later, I began to get an allergic reaction and I called the doctor. She put me on another drug and told me to call her if it got worse.

Physically, I was feeling better, but mentally I wasn't doing well until today. One of my manic drug blood level was low. I feel it is safe to assume that it was either the physical illness or the anti-biotic mixing with the medications that caused me to feel low. I don't want to make this any bigger of an issue than it is, but it is very important to me to explain that physical illnesses cause a lot of strain on the brains of the people who have mental illnesses. I think it was the mix of the medications because I am feeling mentally better about a week after finishing the anti-biotic.

On Sunday, I drove up to Maine to see my good friend Heather. I had gone out with her for about two years and then I decided to break it off. I needed to deal with my life and I decided it was the best decision. We got along really well and got caught up.

Tomorrow I begin my college academic career. Although I shouldn't have, I bought a hat and a backpack. I know I only have one class, but I figured why advertise the fact.

I feel pretty normal today. Once again I pray that it lasts. Peace, for now.

## 29 Jan. 1998

Finally, I woke up at an early time. My sleeping pattern is becoming a little more regular. I was also in a relatively upbeat mood.

I did some errands for my mother and went to the nursing home to see Bea and paint her nails. Although she usually wears red nail polish, I brought a shade of violet and asked her if she liked the color. She seemed pleased so I went ahead and painted her nails that shade. They came out really well. Sometimes it is more difficult to get a near perfect paint job but today was an exception.

I then found myself exhausted and went home and took a nap. I awoke and after lunch I went to pick up my sister at the high school. I was feeling a bit low and wondered how my first day of college would turn out. I dropped my sister off at work and then proceeded to my school to get a temporary ID, books and an application for a parking permit. It soon became more involved than I had planned. I had to make multiple trips to offices, which in turn would send me to other offices, still. The financial aid for my books had not gone through, and since it was the first day of class and I wanted to be prepared I used my credit card.

I then waited in my car for the remainder of the time; keeping warm and smoking cigarettes. Then came the moment I was waiting for. Fifteen minutes before the beginning of the class I began my journey down the unfamiliar sidewalk in the building and up the stairs to room 210. I picked a seat and sat down. The fifteen minutes seemed like an hour. The teacher then arrived and introduced herself, beginning the session with us doing imaginative essays. There were a few awkward moments, but the time went by very quickly. It did not feel like three hours.

So, I am now a college student. How do I feel? Because the class is in the field of English, I am a little excited. I was up until four a.m. this morning before I got to sleep. I visited Sarah and began my homework. It seems like I have a long way to go still with the homework, but I will do a little bit at a time.

Today, I found myself almost in ecstasy. I felt a great sense of peace and well being. My thoughts were however, grounded and logical. I will keep into consideration that when someone is mentally ill they are sometimes the last to know. I do believe; I do believe that today I was actually mentally healthy as opposed to ill. I pray for days like this. I am thankful from my heart.

Everything seems to be in sync. I did however wake up about three p.m., which is something I do not like to do. My sleep schedule is a bit messed up again. It is not that I mind going to bed late and waking up late but it does not work as well with the schedules of the rest of the family. My responsibilities become a little more difficult.

I have hope because of today. The last month was rough and in part why I have a few weeks where I did not write. I wasn't doing terrible but I was symptomatic enough that I felt uncomfortable writing. I had hoped that I would "stay" in my new state of health. I had been told that there will still be rough days. Says when the medication might not work as well. Days like everyone else, mentally ill or not, I experience from time to time. It was at least a reality check. I had two excellent months where I felt well and then I got physically ill and it threw everything out of whack. I hope that today is an indication that things are on the upside again. I will not forget to pray.

## 30 Jan. 1998

FLASHBACK: I was at a church trying to find peace when I decided to go look at the literature in the back of the church. It was the time when I was beginning to be mentally ill and my hands were really bothersome to me from my former work.

This particular day when I was surveying the pamphlets, I was approached by an elderly woman. She said something to the effect of "here, have one of these," or something of the like. What I had been handed was an artists perception of a very young looking Jesus. On the back was a prayer. This prayer however was different from the others. In it was the mention that when my head and hands don't work, help me. I don't remember the exact words but it fit my situation perfectly when I received it. I do not remember the face of the woman, but I'd like to think of her as one of my special angels.

## 04 Feb. 1998

Today before class, I went to the computer lab and worked on the computer for about an hour. The time flew. I then went to class and had a difficult time keeping focused. Part of the problem was probably the lack of food in my system. I had hoped that I had conquered the eating problem. I really thought I had it under control but it is not the case. Yesterday, I had a bagel for breakfast and didn't feel hungry until almost midnight. I then had some tuna along with macaroni. I got sick.

Today I had two pears, a yogurt and a salad. I am fighting to keep it down.

It is not like I don't have food. I budget a healthy breakfast, lunch and dinner, but I'm just not eating. I will keep working at it. Sink or swim.

## 06 Feb 1998

Last night I did laundry and then worked on my homework. It is taking me about 45 minutes per handwritten page to revise and type. After three or four pages I was ready for sleep. It was sometime after four in the morning. I once again altered my sleeping pattern. I do however believe that I am more awake at night. The homework did keep me from drinking alcohol last night. I believe I have my priorities straight.

My last visit with my case manager got me to thinking. She said that I have been blessed by a good angel that watches over me. I have to agree with this. For all the help I have received, I am grateful. Anyway, it got me to thinking how great this angel was. Then I did a reality check. I read somewhere that they (angels) are only servants, not to be praised. I then had a thought that, if they are that great, but not to be praised, we as human beings must hold some significance. I

...And So Am I

must be significant if I am worthy of such help. This is something that I will try not to forget.

On the topic of health, I have been feeling pretty good again. I will try to take good care of myself and try to eat regularly. I have now lost two inches off my waist and am now beginning to look good in my eyes. You are your own worst critic and that definitely holds true with me. Heather told me that I am too self-critical. She is probably right. Out of friendship, I sent her a pair of earrings which I am beginning to believe may have been an error on my part. Although I do not want a relationship, I have been feeling emotions. I do not want a concrete relationship right now because I am still learning a lot. I am hoping she doesn't begin again. I split up with her because I was unhappy with the relationship and seriously believe it was unhealthy. I love her, but I don't want to be the object of obsession. It is something that I am not ready for. I don't know if I will ever be. I guess the jest of this is that I am not wanting a relationship right now. A part of me likes the attention, but part of me feels I must commit to myself first. I am just beginning to feel again.

On 02-05 I went to see my friend, the beautician, and updated my look with two more earrings. I had contemplated this for some time, then was like screw it and I did it. One reason was the fact that I wanted to wear the diamond earring I gave to my grandmother before she passed on. I wanted to feel closer to her. I feel she watches over me from wherever she is now.

Are you still with me? Have I kept your interest? I hope so. (I can write this 'cause I'm the author.) There have been so many changes in my life over the past few years. Some of which is hard to relate to. If you are relating to some of this, I just wish to tell you to hold on. The negative things do pass. Sometimes your brain tells you otherwise, but use your heart. Just look at me. I am just a human being, but I am still here. Somehow the good will shine through. It may be subtle and it may be obvious. Take care for now; me.

...And So Am I

## 06 Feb. 1998

In keeping with a book I read, I saw my index finger appear red, and my middle finger turn green. I thought that it was noteworthy.

## 11 Feb. 1998

Today was a school day. On the 50 minute drive up, I felt a sensation on my left cheek. It was that of a kiss. I then had a "tap" feeling on my left middle finger; the finger of the heart.

## 12 Feb. 1998

I have been reading the beginning of this book and realize how lucky I am. Life is not perfect nor will it probably ever be. I don't mean this in a negative way. I am just being realistic. We need the sorrow to realize joy.

## 13 Feb. 1998

I am presently sitting in my car at the laundromat. It is approximately twelve a.m. I find peace in the early morning hours. Life is a little bit simpler or so it seems. Earlier today (yesterday, technically) I wrote my essay for college basically in one sitting. The only thing I did not like about it was that it jumped around a bit. I will see if I can fix that.

I am a little bit tired although I took naps today to escape a sore throat and chills. My mind however is in pretty good shape. I have the lingering paranoia but other than that I am doing well. I had panic attacks off and on for the last five days but they are beginning to subside.

I have a very hard time with dating and the present pressures that accompany it. I had a wonderful girl who seems to love me very much. I had to take a step back because the relationship was making my life more confusing as opposed to better. There were good things as well, but there were other topics I won't get into that would sometimes

...And So Am I

cause panic attacks. I love her very much; I am just not sure that I am in love with her any more.

I am eating as little as possible in the hope of getting at least a 30 inch waist. The medications I am on and my lack of motivation have a tendency to make one gain weight, which I have. I have gained between three and four inches and have since lost about two of them. I would guess that my waist is a 31 right now. I should be happy with this, but it is not good enough for me.

Today I had a cheeseburger and thought that I was going to loose it. It is either the medications or the fact I have been eating lightly, then pigged out. I have to eat, I do not want to ever go through not being able to sit down again because I had lost so much weight.

### 18 Feb. 1998

It has been a while since I last wrote. I caught a cold and was put on anti-biotic, which have a tendency to mess with my other medications. I began to get symptomatic as the industry puts it, and struggled for a few days. The last few days have left me, at least even, or a little above. I am starting to feel better.

My case manager told me to meditate (or pray) in the morning when I get up. I told her that I pray throughout the day, but she insisted on me praying or meditating first thing in the morning. I don't remember if I prayed this morning for this new test, or just out of habit.

Last night I got a little bit tired. I was outside smoking and I saw a form of a beautiful violet. I then went inside and laid down. I felt energy fill my body. It was a spiritual energy. Did it have anything to do with the "purple" flash? I don't know.

Yesterday, it began to snow pretty heavily. I promised a friend I would stop by for a visit. A little snow was not a major issue for me personally. About 45 minutes after I reach my destination, my mother calls. She said her car was bad in the snow and told me I should pick my sister up at work because my car was front wheel drive and therefore theoretically, better in the snow.

Not that they were great before, but as I drove to pick up my sister the wiper blades on my car literally began to disintegrate. By this time, it was storming pretty heavily and even if I had working wiper blades, it would be difficult to see the road.

The wiper on the passenger side was almost completely shot. The rubber began flipping around like a fish out of water. The driver side wiper began at the bottom and then started to come apart in the middle where my line of vision was.

I was anxious, but not really afraid. I did however picture myself with my car wrapped around a telephone pole. I then began a prayer. I don't know the exact words but I know I asked for help. I was patient. I did not know what the answer would be or when I would receive it.

About three minutes passed and the driver side wiper began to clear the windshield so that I could see the road; of what could be seen.

Was this another of my Angelic interventions or merely coincidence? In either case I was blessed. I made the trip safely.

### 19 Feb. 1998

Just a quick note before I forget. I have been making myself consciously focus and try to be patient.

I am presently at the laundromat, drying my clothes for the week. I have to work tomorrow so I have to do laundry today; work clothes included.

Right now I am feeling very confused. I do not think it should be replaced with overwhelmed although I am feeling a little bit of that as well.

I then go back to the issue of patience. I am trying to do all of my work, studies and recreation all at the same time. I need to learn to pace myself.

Today I woke up. I do not remember if I prayed like my case manager suggested, but I think I at least thought of it. I believe this is a

...And So Am I

start. My early morning mental state was a bit cloudy, but I was in a pretty good mood.

I then went to work and picked up my paycheck. I did my usual errands: food, coffee, nicotine and gas. I then went to a discount store to see if they still had their recycled jeans. I had seen on my last visit a pair of grungy 30's that the first time I saw them, I knew I would never fit into them. My waist is down to about that now, so I decided to take a look. I found the pair (for the record, the others were clean with wear) of stained jeans with a worn spot where the previous owner kept a can of chew. Somewhere in my fashion conscious mind, I felt this particular pair had a place. The pants had been worn by someone who either worked or played hard. To me they were like a piece of history. My mother said I'd probably get crabs. I tried them on. They were a bit snug, but they fit. I believe I have another inch or so to go. Even though it is wrong to suppose that then, I will feel good about myself. I will be a little closer to the person I was before I got sick. I do already feel a little bit better. It is not how much I weigh, but rather how I perceive I look to the world. I am trying very hard not to create or recreate an eating disorder. I do however feel very guilty for eating a bag of chips today.

Today I had a nonfat yogurt, two pears, five bagels and a bag of chips. Ideally, I would have preferred to have a pair instead of the chips.

I think this may be an obsessive behavior, not a disorder, but I am not a doctor. Perhaps, if I ate a little better the confusion might go away. I do not really know. Growing up I would eat off and on and had sporadic eating patterns for a host of different reasons. Sometimes I was picky. I guess it is still there it just shifted a little.

**20 Feb. 1998**

I am trying again to master patience. I am at the psychiatrist's office waiting for my turn to regurgitate information, which may be of use to my cause.

Last night around midnight, I added a can of tuna and another pear. This created a sense of guilt; but I don't ever want to get too small. The carbohydrates equaled guilt, but I feel like I needed the protein.

## 22 Feb. 1998

I have been bingeing and purging. By purging, I mean not eating. It does not bother me any more to throw up. (Like needles, I am beginning to get used to it.) Not that it is something I enjoy either. I think it is safe to assume that I probably would not ever willfully cause myself to vomit. I ask the powers that be to bless the food I eat. I therefore would not feel right to do the aforementioned act. My medications sometimes make me sick, I am getting used to it. It is becoming less frequent. Even my hair has been falling out at a much lesser rate.

Right now I am at work popping corn in the popping room. I think they believe I like popping corn. I guess it is not that bad if I can listen to music and read or write; between batches waiting for the corn to explode.

Tonight I am scheduled to work an odd shift. It is halfway between the morning and evening shifts. When I get out, whether it is at the scheduled eight p.m. or earlier (which is a possibility because we have plenty of corn), I intend to go to the computer lab at the college and finish typing my essay. Much to my dismay, the school computer accepts my home computer format, but the home computer will not accept the school format. Hence the need for the 50 minute drive. Tonight the computer lab is supposed to be open until midnight. I figure I can make it there by ten p.m. and will have a good two hours to work on the essay. I might be able to finish it. Doubtful, but possible. If I don't finish it tonight, I will have to go tomorrow to complete it.

I am in a reasonably good mood today. I was in a good mood last night. I have my share of stressors to be sure, but I am at least a little above the "blah" line. This is a good thing.

Yesterday while visiting a friend, we went for a ride to the video store nearby. We soon learned we did not have the same taste in mov-

...And So Am I

ies. The majority of the ones we did agree upon we had already seen. Finally, we both agreed on an old 80's flick. I had seen it before and was a little unsettled, but not too badly. In this movie, the murderer turns out to be the schizophrenic that nobody likes. I know that something like this would never happen in this day and age. I know that it was an older movie, but it made me a little angry. They made fun of this kid, he starts killing people, he gets killed and everyone lives happily ever after. Is this a cliché, or what? Any stereotyping here? I will not say, imply, or intend that some mentally ill people do not have irrational thoughts. Some do. I know I did. I feel this movie was inaccurate however, because 10% of the time a schizophrenic will die from either suicide or accidental death. One in ten. So far I have been lucky. I myself, personally, would be far more likely to attempt suicide than to commit homicide. This is not to say that either by voices or irrational thoughts that it has never come up. It has. I had enough intelligence to say "No," or "Stop it" or other means of self talk. For me, however unpleasant, have had really bad thoughts that were beyond my control. All I could do is to let go; let them pass. It is at times as if I have two brains. I mean this quite literally. It was like, "Do this," "No." Sometimes I would feel guilt for having these thoughts. Now presently, I am experiencing a relatively small amount of bad thoughts, and I now accept them for what they are. I usually don't get upset as of late, but it can be trying all the same. Anyway, I know I would not kill another.

I try to stay away from triggers – things that tend to set off irrational thoughts. For me the most common triggers are items such as biblical writing, children, newspapers and television (especially, the news). Some activities that don't usually trigger unwanted responses are movies, books and driving.

It probably is no wonder then that I am more likely to have triggers if I have other symptoms; especially slight to moderate depression. This is when I am below the "blah" line.

I am not ashamed of my illness. I do at times get upset from irrational thoughts, which in turn creates a cycle. I get down, then am more likely to become once again symptomatic.

I guess all in all, what I wish to close with today is that, of the contact that I have had with the mentally ill, in the hospital and those I have met on the street have maybe been a little eccentric, but on the whole, very nice, well mannered people. The schizophrenics in this case - they were too inward and preoccupied to do any harm to others. These particular schizophrenics also in turn would be more apt to get hit by a car on the street, than to harm anyone else. This is my observation.

### 23 Feb. 1998

Yesterday I got tipped a dollar. Why? Was the cost of the concession not enough? I am very curious since this is the first time I had been tipped. It has almost been three years that I've worked in this building. I know I am doing the best I can with the new policies, but was it worth a dollar? The coffee I now sip is courtesy of a stranger.

### 01 Mar. 1998

I am feeling a little low today. More likely than not it is because I drank alcohol last night, despite the fact that I am not supposed to drink with my medications. I have now lost about three inches off my waist. Now I have to start motivating myself and do sit-ups. Although I have not been strict with it, I believe my diet has a lot to do with my recent and rapid weight loss. Am I happy with my current size? Yes and no. I feel a little happiness in the fact I am conquering the weight gain side-effects of my medication. I am however still longing to possess a model's physique. It is a reality I believe I can accomplish. It is in part because I went through modeling school and was told on more than one occasion that I had a "gut." To someone who was already very conscious, this phrase has had a lasting impact. I know that I was at the recommended "ideal" weight, gut and all; so now I am probably

...And So Am I

a bit under. I am not prone to gaining muscle. I worked out at the gym and had very little results. It is then why I chose to lose weight by diet. I have a curl bar and an abdominal machine at home. As I have stated earlier, I just have to use them.

My illness has been pretty stable. I have been quite emotional, however. This is a good thing, but I have been wanting to cry almost every day out of frustration. Some of what I am dealing with now are just things I would be dealing with, illness or not. I honestly cannot remember what I dealt with before I got sick. It has been a long time; I am feeling pretty good. I guess it is basically stress of school, work and life in general. I have been dealing pretty well and take the stress medication as infrequently as possible. I am allotted about four a month and have been taking one or two in that time-span.

Then we come back to emotions. I am not used to them and have sadly been looking for any legal escape I can find. I am praying that I will not be tempted to drink alcohol tonight. I don't think I have the makings of an alcoholic, although I can honestly say I can understand some of the reasoning behind alcoholism. I have been "using" it frequently as an escape from my mind. I have cut down my nicotine intake. Unfortunately, I am not good at regulating it, so we will have to see where this goes.

I am just sick of fighting the illness, even though I know I must. I have come so far. I wish I could take pride in this fact, but somehow I cannot. I don't know if it is my comparison to my former self, or that of others. It is becoming increasingly rare for someone to ask me what is wrong. This fact alone shows our progress. I pluralized the last sentence on purpose. There is the help of the doctor, counseling by my therapist, general help with anything by my case manager and lastly, but not least, the higher powers that Be. All of these people have played a significant roll in helping me to overcome the illness. I still have symptoms but my dependence on these people have been diminished a lot. I seem to be keeping my own lately.

My mind is pretty clear now and I am doing all my homework for school. My stress level has been up and down but has also for the most part stabilized. I am and probably always will be emotional. The manic phases have been mostly under control. Why then, am I still not convinced of my self worth?

I guess it is the memories that, if forgotten, might give me peace. I cannot forget them; they are a part of me. How then can I learn to accept the past and put it behind me? I have replaced most of my material goods in an effort to forget. I has helped a little, but material goods are just that. No more, no less.

I long for the peace of mind (and sometimes, body inclusive) that I get from time to time. Sometimes it is for a few moments, other times longer; possibly an hour or two. It is a sense that every thing is going to be okay. This is why I have been bingeing on nicotine, caffeine and to some extent alcohol. I am trying to create the peace, but it does not take a scientist to realize that it doesn't happen (usually) that way.

The peace is the opposite of guilt. The guilt of the things I thought or did while I was sick. My mind would replay the offending memories over and over like a CD on repeat, or it would just spit it out at random in the least opportune moments. This has slowed down a little, but since my memory itself is getting better, I am once again faced with guilt; guilt and fear. I imagine I will learn to overcome this in time. Until then, I will be the best man I can be.

Since attending school, I have noticed a change in my brain patterns. My ability to reason and memory has improved somewhat. Although my mind is still a little muddled, I have for the most part been able to keep up and comprehend most of the materials given. I guess it is an acceptance of however my mind is and then, "Okay, here's what I have to do." So far this has been working. For three hours a week I try to bypass the schizo-affective disorder and become a college student. At this particular moment I am feeling apprehension about my performance. I know in my heart that I am doing my best. I guess it goes back to the question of self worth. Could my own work ever be good enough for myself?

## 03 Feb. 1998

I am noticing a pattern. The cycle begins. I rationally create an offense or memories of mistakes play at random. I become very upset and just feel a sense of unworthiness. This being, either or both: society or my higher power. I punish myself in any way I can. Whether it is not eating/bingeing, alcohol, overdoses of over-the-counter stimulants or nicotine abuse. I am not proud of this cycle I am in and am doing my best to end it. At least curb the abuses. Am I still functioning? Yes. Does the abuse leave me feeling any better? I don't believe so. Why do it then, you ask. I believe it is because I don't have "control" of my life; I have control over the substances and the abuse. I guess it is part of the cycle. I am now starting to get to the end of this circle, or so it feels. I used to have these symptoms in a much more concentrated form before the mood-med. Tomorrow, I could wake up and be back to myself again. I can pray.

I might be able to break this cycle with a sedative. I want to add that I do not abuse my prescription medications. They are sacred somehow. I do not want to break the trust with my doctor.

## 03 Mar. 1998

I wish I could remember when I wrote my last entry. It must have been between early morning and 3:30 PM yesterday. The point of the last statement was that I saw my case manager at 3:30. I will take into consideration that it was late in the afternoon and she being my most favored drive towards health gives her credibility. Anyway, I told her about my current bingeing and she basically voiced that I was deliberately trying to sabotage my recovery. I love her very much, but that is crap.

In anger over the last 24 hours, I had to think about it. I pondered this possibility. I came to the conclusion that it is definitely not the case. In fact, upon ending (for the most part) my bingeing I have actually come to peace. It has been some time since I had it, but in my opinion this fact emphasizes that I do not wish, even subconsciously, to be anything but at peace. I am grateful, Thanks.

Earlier today, I discovered that I was in front of a police car. Slowing a few miles per hour, I pulled into the left lane because I was going to be turning left. I got into the left lane and put on the cruise control, as to not speed. I saw the police car on my right side, then hang back and got behind me. Although there should have been no reason for me to be pulled over, completely sober, I fumbled to get my license. He said I was following too close to the car in front of me (when I shifted lanes there was no one in front of me) and that I swerved going through the intersection. He then insulted me by asking if I put [drugs] on the floor. It was not a pleasant experience, but I knew it was borderline harassment. I think he was hoping for a ticket or an arrest to add to his collar. This is my belief. Not all police are like that, for the record. I have just found that more are, than not.

## 05 Mar. 1998

I came up with a morning prayer:

"Although I feel okay today, God please help me through this day."

## 07 Mar. 1998

I wanted to take a minute to recap the day. I woke up today with a hangover like sick feeling. I was scheduled to work at three, so I forced myself to take a shower. I thought I was going to be sick so I went to lie down. I ran downstairs to the bathroom, but beginning to feel a little better, I then went back to lie down. I fell asleep and didn't wake up until three. I called work and explained to them that I overslept. I was not reprimanded but instead was told to get there as soon as possible, that I was needed.

...And So Am I

I drove to work in a daze. I arrive at work about 45 minutes late. I immediately jump right into work. Without my caffeine fix (my stomach was still a bit queasy) I somehow managed to do all right.

I was then sent up to pop corn. I slowly sipped the coffee and had my usual breakfast. What is the worst that could happen? Something amazing happened. I began to actually feel better. The whole rest of my shift went very peaceably with only a couple of spats of emotional upset, which I was able to overcome with ease; somehow.

I leave work still at peace. I was not euphoric, but rather in a state of well-being. I drive home cautious as not to speed or swerve. (It is a fact that I tend to go faster when I am in a good mood.) Upon arriving home, I feel a little cautious. Not that there was really anything to worry about, but I just didn't want anything to disrupt the peace I felt.

I go in. Mom and Dad were asleep and my younger brother, who never ceases to come up with little things to irritate me, was still up. I went downstairs and worked on my homework while my laundry was in the wash. I take a break and go upstairs to bring a video up. He had turned all the lamps off (because they were his and he didn't want me to disturb him). I don't know. I then took my clothes out of the washing machine and drove to the Laundromat. I am still at peace. I discover someone has left a couple of tabloids, which I am proud to say, I no longer believe everything that I read. I chose to read the rags over the present book I am reading about relationships and the philosophy and psychology of them. I drive home and sit in my car. I pray for the people that I felt needed it. On different days, I pray for different people. I don't have any usual routine – just when I am well and up to it, I send my love. It is now 3:21 AM and I am exhausted, but I am still in a peaceful mood. Once again, I must thank everyone (and there are many) who have helped me in my life.

## 07 Mar. 1998

Today I had a good day until about 6:30 or 7:00 PM. I then lay down to try and wait for the panic to pass. By 7:45 it still had not subsided so I took a sedative. Then I began however, to have dim visions, much like a dream. Two I remember clearly – one was of myself looking down at my steering wheel. The other was the nightstand belonging to my brother with a phone and alarm clock on it. At first I thought I was just spacing out, looking at it, and then I opened my eyes and could see nothing in the dark.

## 09 Mar. 1998

Yesterday was a pretty good day. I felt a little weak and shaky on the physical realm, but mentally was pretty strong. Today is the third day in a row that I have felt pretty good since my "bad cycle." The day is still young yet, but it is already in my book, classified as a good day.

A good day is a day where I am relatively at peace. It can include happiness, but it does not necessarily mean happiness.

## 10 Mar. 1998

Upon revising my writings, I have noticed a considerable evolution. I have edited it as I have gone along, but some of my writing has been in part left alone because it reflects my writings before I began to feel better.

It may or may not have been mentioned that the antibiotics altered the effectiveness of my other medications and that I had to work a little harder at being well. Also, over-the-counter medications have a similar effect. Since I had an infection (which already seriously altered my mood, as with almost any virus or infection), I was later finding myself in a self-destructive cycle, which I am finally getting out of. When I am self-destructive, I do not write as a rule. It is generally too difficult; and negative. Now that I am getting over it, writing is much simpler. It can be documented as an obsessive-compulsive behavior. Not necessarily a disorder, just a behavior. As I have written earlier about leaving negatives alone, I too must learn to leave things out of place, alone.

...And So Am I

In the recent past, I have been punishing myself for not being "perfect" or living up to my own standards, which are probably in all reality, unrealistic. I have been doing so by excessive amounts of caffeine, nicotine, alcohol and over-the-counter stimulants. It has now subsided and I have less desire to purge in these ways. My eating, however, is a different story.

Although I know that I am now at a good weight for my size, I still want to lose just a little more. "One more inch," I tell myself, "then you'll be happy with yourself." I ask myself then, will one more inch actually make that much difference? I know, rationally and medically, it is necessary to eat. I know that eating helps to regulate the medications. Why then, do I find myself still torturing myself with not eating well? As I stated earlier, I do not want to ever get to the point where it hurts to sit down. I guess this is something I will have to think about on a rational level. One thing I once again want to make clear is that I don't care how much I weigh. It is how my mind perceives how I look. I had a fleeting thought, in God's eyes, does this make me vain?

This morning (after I slept), I had something very strange happen. The easiest way to describe the state I was in – sleepwalking. I was awake, but somewhat unaware of what I was doing at the time. In this particular instance I found myself taking off all my jewelry that I had been collecting as symbols of achievement, instances where I grew out of part of my illness. I then woke up confused and wondering why I had taken them off.

The first hour of the day was filled with irrational thoughts and involuntary lack of focus. I was also very sluggish motivation-wise. Today, I start a new job at work. I will be selling tickets, along with concession. Even though I am unmotivated, I will take a shower and get ready for today.

I took a shower and feel a little better.

Today in general I am feeling a bit low, and am finding it difficult to concentrate. I can't complain however, because I had about four good, peaceful days in a row.

I have been feeling and seeing lots of colors today. I have been praying a lot today, maybe it is their answer. I am seeing purple, green, blue and a little bit of orange. I am very emotional today so far. This emotional turmoil has lessened some as the day progressed, but I am still quite not at peace in my emotional state.

I have also discovered that my job is making me "obsessive-compulsive." At school, I felt that I had to pick the paper towels off the floor. All in all, this may not be a terrible discovery. I just hope that it doesn't progress into an "illness."

## 11 Mar. 1998

I woke up before eight a.m. this morning and started my daily routine. I was in a better mood than yesterday, but was a little tired still, so I went back upstairs and took a nap. I am willing to bet that I needed to sleep a little more because of the medications that do make me drowsy. Also, I have always, sick or well, needed eight to nine hours of sleep a night.

Upon awakening, at about 11:45, I was experiencing another vision. This time it was of a window. I tried to, although I cannot explain, prolong the vision so that it might make sense to me. I prolonged it for about two seconds, or was allowed to see it for that time. Making little sense, I went downstairs and told my mother what I had just experienced and she said, "Look out the window, Nate got his car stuck in the mud out back." Was this the meaning for the window vision? Could be.

About six o'clock, a half hour before class, I began to get emotionally overwhelmed. I can't really explain it, but it felt as though I was turning inside out. I didn't know what to do, so I went back to my car and started to pray for help. About five minutes later, I started to feel better; the emotions started to pass. By 6:15, I was ready to go to class. I made it to the class. I socialized and left feeling a bit tired, but I was glad I made it through.

...And So Am I

## 12 Mar. 1998

12:00 a.m. I am at peace, but a little edgy.

Today, I woke up feeling low and decided I would take control of the situation because the psychiatrist is only available on certain days. I then called my primary care physician and asked her if I could have some blood work done to check the levels of medications in my system. I don't know why, but sometimes the levels go down. I have had many good days in a row and all of a sudden, I started getting symptomatic. That is why I asked to get the lab work done. (I still don't like needles.)

At school, I am making friends and not even trying. I wish that I could be able to, and allow myself to see the good things that I do. Do I not want to? Is it my own mind that won't allow this? Is it conditioning? All of the above? If I did experience self-esteem would it get out of hand? Would I lose control?

## 13 Mar. 1998

It is now two in the morning, Eastern Standard Time, and I am starting to feel at peace again. I am a little uneasy, but for the most part, feeling well. I wish to take a moment to explain that almost all of the side effects from my medications have largely disappeared. In that respect, I feel pretty "normal." I am still not pacing. I look healthy. Once in a while I get the shakes but, it has only been a couple of times that it was so bad I couldn't write. I am not rocking.

The doctors try to get me "even." I think personally that it is better to have a little bit of emotion, good and bad.

I woke up with a "med-head," or medicine hangover. In itself, it does not bother me because usually, they only last an hour or so and then I am usually in a really good mood for the rest of the day.

About three hours passed after I woke up and I still had a mild, yet annoying headache. This phenomenon is rare. I took a pain-reliever and went to work. I am feeling better.

**29 Mar. 1998**

My blood work came back low, but in range. I asked my psychiatrist if I could increase my dose of the anti-depressant. He okayed it. The increase has only been for a few days now. Usually, the actual results take about or between two and four weeks. I have found, although I am having mood-swings, that I am having less of the low side.

**FLASHBACK:**

When I was under ten years of age, I had a recurring dream in which I was kidnapped by a woman with a bandana on her head. The woman was not particularly cruel, but was not entirely kind either. She would take a stone and place it on my throat in a swiping manner. This act then took my voice and I could not scream. I remember vividly trying, but to no avail. I do not remember much more of the dream, but she later restored my voice and I, either by waking up or by some other means, returned to my family. I believe that the vagueness of the ending, aside from time elapsed, was that it had different endings. Perhaps, once, I escaped.

The reason I brought this dream up is because she used a stone to take away my voice. I just thought it was odd that, as a child, I had an experience with a dream in which someone used a crystal for ill reasons. I also find it of interest that as a child, stones had meanings. Although, I had "special" rocks, basically just for sentiment when I was young, it was not until much later in life that I learned about the metaphysical properties of stones and minerals.

**25 Mar. 1998**

I have been trying to keep school outside of my writing, but I have come to the conclusion that it is now a part of my life. Although it is only one class, it has become so much more.

Today, I did my usual errands and then went to school to attend a support group of people like myself. I did not find myself uncomfort-

...And So Am I

able; at least not any more than usual. There were a couple of clients who were tapping and making noise. Abnormally, I found this bothersome, which was probably part of the cause for the slight discomfort.

I then went to an academic support person who asked me how I was doing; and she was interested in my work. It was approximately three hours before I had class, so I went to a shop where they sold crystals. I found a stone that jumped out at me. They labeled it "Blood Agate" after the blood-like spats on the stone. Feeling a kin for this stone, I forfeited my coffee money without regret.

Today, as with last week, I had a stress-manic-panic attack, which I decided to work through without medication.

Class went well. My interview with my boss was approved of by the class. My title, "Interview with a Vampire" stood out. I figured that since I was dealing with the movie business, then I would give it a spin on a movie title.

Despite all the pain and frustration, I really do love my life. The turquoise cloudless sky shown amidst comfortably tolerable temperature made for a beautiful day. I fell asleep on the front porch staring at the sky wondering about the wisdom of the universe. There was a certain peace.

## 29 Mar. 1998

I have been working non-stop for the last three days. Today will make number four. I have been quite emotional lately for various reasons and therefore been glad to work to take my mind off the emotional pain. Working for me is tough, but it has proven to be a good thing. I have still been popping corn, but have also been on concession, register, "shoveling," corn and have been entrusted to selling tickets of which I have found to be somewhat pleasurable – the closest thing to my previous job, basically non-existent, of tearing tickets.

I went home yesterday (it is now 1:30 PM) pretty much at peace and tired, so I tried to get some sleep. I don't believe I actually got any sleep, but I had an unusual vision while lying down. In this particular insight, I saw a tunnel of white light, which somehow seemed "padded" and I could not see the end. Around the tunnel that seemed to move but did not, there were what appeared to be stars. I do not know what if anything this vision meant. My personal thoughts on it were that maybe this is where my prayers go. I really don't know. There is so much room for interpretation and my mind can only decipher so much of it. I did however find peace in the vision although the reason for it and the meaning escapes me. I had felt however that my Grandmother was still with me. As usual I went with a thought. It was selfish to some degree to keep her here with me when I know she deserved to be with her husband, and her savior. I prayed that if my Grandma was still here that she find the light and go to it. I am unsure of the outcome.

A few days ago I had an increase in my anti-depressant medication. I asked for it. I have been kind of manic-like in symptoms lately. I have been "crashing" again. Manic-drug blood level wise I am low, but in range. In exact I am a .6%, which is the lowest of the desired range. The range is from .6% to 1.2%. I have been finding myself happy or content then blank or passively suicidal. For reasons unknown to myself I feel as though I want to die although I probably would never do it (and this is a definite maybe). I do love my life, but at times overwhelmed emotionally or flooded with memories since my "rebirth" when I got sick, the present, and the garbage of the past. For the most part this is something that emotionally and rationally I have to learn to deal with. I partly attribute this new wave of emotion to my new anti-psychotic medication which has given me certain mental and emotional freedom that I have not experienced since I became ill and was medicated heavily for certain symptoms. I find myself crying or happy for no apparent reason. I must learn to deal with this.

Five p.m. I was on a manic high when I arrived at work. A few hours later I crashed and it has slowly but steadily been worsening. My blood level of the anti-manic drug was low on the desired range. I am afraid an increase will give me more side effects. At this point I

...And So Am I

don't know which is worse. It is like my former fear of needles (not that I especially like them now), which began after about seven shots to numb my jaw at the dentist's office when I was a child. One of my baby teeth did not fall out and my adult teeth were growing straight out like fangs.

"A little pinch," was succeeded by another – each one making me more squeamish, it didn't hurt bad, but was a really gross feeling. The point of the last two paragraphs was to help describe how I feel now. I am trying to be strong, courageous and appreciative of my life and this world. I am thankful. However, like the shots of Novocain many years ago these pangs of upsetedness are making it extremely difficult to want to survive. The warrior in me keeps pushing me, but how long can he hold out? It is not really a depression, but a low following mania coupled with low self-esteem and self-worth. I have been fighting for my identity severely. Nothing in particular but everything in general. I guess the line between eclectic and no identity has been entwined and I am having a difficult time with it. Who are my peers? What style of music do I listen to? What kind of books/magazines do I read? I must tell you it is like being born a second time, memories overlap; they seldom fade away.

## 31 Mar. 1998

I have been abstaining from over-the-counter stimulants and alcohol for the last few weeks. I was told it could be aggravating my condition, although I was using as a means to "find the peace" that I had felt and now was no longer feeling. After a call to my mental health clinic my anti-depressant and stress medication dosages was increased. The only problem I had was the way I was treated over the phone by one of my two counselors. She said in effect that I was creating my symptoms, and that was all we talked about, that we "were at the beginning again." This greatly upset me and after I hung up the phone, in an empty house, I screamed as loud as I could. Again, there,

I was a little better but not much. I did everything that I was "supposed to do." It didn't work.

Today so far, so good. I am hoping that today yields the great peace I felt last night. I didn't want to go to sleep and let it be wasted. If my experience has taught me anything it is what my prevailing moods will be like. It is not to say there is never an occasional curve ball, but for the most part it is at least 75% predictable. I am learning slowly the triggers. It is not foolproof, however. Today by how I feel, I will either have a pretty good day or I may crash and get upset. My bet is on a good day.

## 03 Apr. 1998

Today I feel a great peace. It is both a physical and emotional/mental peace. I feel, for this brief period, forgiven for that which I cannot even forgive myself for. Anyone else might find the offenses trivial. It is perhaps one of life's subtle lessons that I should lighten up a little.

## 04 Apr. 1998

It is eight a.m. and I am the only one awake in the whole house. Although my mind is a little bit scattered at the present, I have used my mantra and prayed for help throughout the day. The last five or so days have been very peaceful, both physically and mentally, since the increases in my medications.

I got my check yesterday and paid my bills; loan repayments, credit card payments and some other odds and ends including a hundred dollars I set aside for car repair. (My muffler is shot, and my temperature sensor is not working.)

I then had about fifty dollars left. I paid the above bills before my 11:30 psychiatrist appointment. Nothing spectacular. He asked me if I had been drinking or doing any stimulants or other drugs. I told him honestly that it had been about a month. I hope that I showed him I was at least working on curbing the self-medication and abuse.

Then, as I planned, I headed to the city where I presently go to school. The psychiatrist's office is ten miles from my home. The city is twenty miles from the doctor's office. Anyway, I went to the city to purchase a book that I could not find anywhere else. I also bought a few candles, some stones, and a blue aqua aura pendant, which is at the present, residing next to the cross around my neck.

The owner of the shop had a conversation with me. I showed him the stones I had collected and asked him if there was any stone that might be beneficial. He then ushered me into the office in the back of the shop and dumped a large basket of stones on his desk. He picked out a few and handed them one at a time to me. He then gave me three stones. I asked him how much they were and he said not to worry about it. My guess is they were worth, give or take, seven dollars. I spent enough money to make me eligible for a free Beanie Baby. I felt a need to name it, so I named it Gabe, after the Arch Angel Gabriel.

I am still buying videos, mostly used, for my collection. As with movies, I am going through a period where I am not interested as much as I used to or would like to be.

**09 Apr. 1998**

Some of my writing is at times a bit dark, some positive and some things I felt worthy of mention. I wish to give you a gift. The following poem is one that I wrote, approximately in 1990, about four years before I got sick. I hope it brings you a moment of peace that I tried to envision while writing it.

Take you to a place,
It's not very far—
Won't go on foot,
Don't need a car—
Prejudice is gone, melted away,
The sun it shines indefinitely—
The air is sweet; there is no time,

No worried thoughts, no boggled minds—
Toxic waste does not exist,
The ozone has no holes—
Fear not of war it is not here,
No age nor death of loved ones dear—
For now this journey soon must end—
Until we meet again my friend—

**FLASHBACK:**

I am in the first grade. The teacher devised a game for us in part to soak up a little extra sun, also to teach us about "evolution" and the food chain. In this game the teacher had marked empty milk cartons with numbers on them from 1 to 5, if my memory serves me. She scattered the milk boxes around the playground. We were given instructions: some of the animals were allowed to run. Others had to walk. And I, for a reason still unknown to myself, was elected to hop on one leg to symbolize an injured animal. Needless to say, I did not get any of the milk boxes, and she explained that in the wild, injured animals didn't survive as well as the healthy ones. I was told that others did not survive at all.

Why she chose me to be the injured beast, I don't know. But in retrospect, I don't believe that this game did much for a child that did not have a great deal of self-esteem to begin with. I understand it was just a game, but to me, I feel that she could have chosen someone who had, quite frankly, a better self-esteem.

The memory is not terrible. I had fun trying to get the "food" but, for me, the pangs of the memory remains.

**13 Apr. 1998**

It is now about 11:00 pm. I fell asleep peaceably around 4 pm and woke up around ten. I usually do not care much to throw off my sleeping pattern, but as stated earlier, I am at peace for the first time in weeks, so I am happy.

I am sitting in my car writing, staring, at the moon in all its splendor…It is full tonight.

The last few days found me in angst and I needed to lash out. It was an emotional lash as opposed to one in specific anger. If it was anger, which is rare, it was directed to myself. I was uncomfortable with my human flaws and wanted and needed a change before I hurt myself.

I have lost quite a bit of weight, for me, despite the known weight increase from the medications. With this, I am pleased because I think I look good. Not muscular and toned as I wish, but I am thin and flat.

My only concern with the weight loss is, although I have been bingeing on occasion, I am counting calories, and although I have plenty of food, I am not eating it. My average caloric intake not including beverages is about a thousand a day.

I also lashed out and dyed my hair. It was okay, but it had no shock value so it was useless to my cause. I re-dyed it, still not the results I had hoped for. I then opted for bleach. My sister spends over a hundred dollars getting her hair bleached, I figured I could do it myself and save a chunk of change.

My hair came out orange. Not just a little red, but orange! I had to work the next day, so I felt I needed to do something. I bought two dyes one was blonde and the other light brown. I used the blonde first and while it was wet I was quite pleased with the colour. I went to bed. I then woke up and had a crash course in hair colouring. When your hair is wet, it is a different shade. I looked in the mirror and it was orange again! Somewhat muted, but still orange. I had an hour before work so I, now being the professional hair colourist (ha ha), got out and mixed the brown together. I applied it. It said to leave it on for 25 minutes. I washed it out after 20 minutes. Still orange. It was muted enough to be acceptable, but orange, the same.

One of the people I work with came in to see a movie and told me my hair, "Looked like shit." He didn't need to tell me what I already knew. I then decided, much to the dismay of my scalp and hair I was going to get the orange out. By this trial, I had spent at least what it would cost to have it professionally done.

I bleached it again. This time I left it in a little longer. It came out platinum blond with orange hi-lights. By this time, I didn't have great aspirations to being a blond anymore; at least not for the time being. I went to the 24 hour pharmacy and spent about an hour comparing hair shades, common results and compatibility.

This time I got it right. I picked out a brand advertised by a highly regarded star, and made the attempt to fix my orange problem. (It is not to say I don't like red or orange hair, just that it is not good for me. I was now a little seasoned in the hair colouring field, and although had secretly hoped for finding a deep ash brown, darker than my natural color, I chose a light gold brown which actually was quite similar to my hair in the sunlight, or how it looked in the summer. I was pleased. My scalp was not, however. I kept the phrase my sister in California told me in mind. "It hurts to be beautiful." In this instance, although I would have chosen the word normal over beautiful, I seriously knew what she meant.

## 19 Apr. 1998

At the present, I feel well. Although I have not eaten yet today, it is still early. I ate relatively well yesterday. I have largely stopped eating and was frustrated that I would get "sick" again. I have been clean, with no alcohol or over the counter stimulants and the like, for almost two months. Although this was not difficult to end, I have been in tremendous mental pain lately. It is not like the pain of a headache. For that, a couple of pain relievers usually do the trick. It is rather, an overwhelming pain that I would have probably con-sumed alcohol to dull. It is a pain of frustration and of anguish. It is not easily described.

I am down to about a 29-inch waist. I am happy with my current size, but do not know how much food, to maintain it. I have not been very physical, so too many calories would turn into excess flesh. I

...And So Am I

wish I could be more muscular and defined, but in fact I went to the gym off and on, and honestly had close to no results.

As for the mental pain and correlating panic, I have tried my best to use the stress medication as sparingly as possible. Last night, I took an additional panic-medication in the hope that the pain would be relieved and I would have a good nights' sleep. The results: I still woke up early, but I felt all right. I guess clinically, I would be regarded as doing well, for the most part. I do however, long for the mental peace. The physical peace generally accompanies it.

Last night, although friends had told me it wasn't a good idea, I was frustrated and bought a light ash brown dye and coloured my hair. That makes three bleachings and seven colourings within two weeks. I am however, more comfortable with the darker shade that is a bit darker than my natural colour. It gave me a little peace. I like it.

On 17 Apr. 98, I received a response letter I wrote to a band. It had only been a week since I wrote to them, but they sent me a lithograph with each band members signatures and also, a band greeting card which was addressed to me, with the band name and date, peace (which was reciprocated from my letter) and all the band members signatures. This material came on one of my bad days (the Lord works in mysterious ways), which although being very emotionally up and down, presented little comfort.

### 23 Apr. 1998

Yesterday, I overslept and woke up with a med-head hangover. It was a little worse than usual, so I took a pain reliever, over the counter. I then went about my business before class. I saw my case manager because I had stopped eating and literally gagged when attempting to eat. I asked for help.

As usual, and I am not sure why, after the headache goes away, I have a really good day.

I was almost in ecstasy, almost total piece of mind, body and spirit. I prayed.

## 01 May 1998

I received some stickers, a guitar pick and a note from a quite prominent band. It was quite a surprise, and the note basically said to take things as they come. Things will fall together; thanks for your love and support.

This letter actually brought me comfort; it made me feel less alone in this world despite friends.

My moods recently have been pretty much on the upper blah level. I have been experiencing brief and longer periods of peace. I have been a little panicky, but not terribly bad. I am seriously blessed in that I can see glimpses of beauty and wonder. Yesterday, while on the porch, just chilling out before a meeting, I saw a yellow butterfly. It was so beautiful and emotionally I was almost brought to tears. I said a quick prayer, and asked the powers if I could see the butterfly up close. Almost as if on cue, the brightly coloured butterfly flew about 100 feet, flew by me, and did a U-turn and flew close enough that I could almost touch him. Coincidence or no, it was a work of beauty. I thanked my God.

## 02 May 1998

On weekends, getting my mind together for work, I go out on the porch and have a cigarette or two. It is probably not a good habit, but usually the coffee and cigarettes appear to help me focus somewhat. Anyway, as I sit there and smoke (the porch being a good 10 to 15 feet from the garage below), I once in a while see my father or other family member pop out of the garage door, as the chipmunks do, for whatever task they set out to do.

...And So Am I

## 03 May 1998

The last few days, about 3 or 4, I have been sleeping relatively well and waking up in a good mood. I am at peace; overall. However, what goes up must come down, and in the course of the day, albeit somewhat normal for a flux of feelings and emotions, mine are much more persistent, to be sure. On 01 May 98, I had to take a sedative because I was getting low and began to panic. I feel this was justified, despite the fact I try not to take any more medicine than needed.

Right now, I will be thankful for the peace it brings. As always, it is appreciated.

## 14 May 1998

"To thine own self be true..." - William Shakespeare

I just took my socks off and walked barefoot comfortably to my car, opened my backpack and began writing. I wanted to write today because I feel at ease with myself, and the world. I feel great.

I now weigh 134 pounds and am happy at the weight. I am however going to my doctor today to rule out medical reasons why I have lost 30 lbs. Ten pounds in the last two weeks.

I have been working on eating and although I feel bloated or sick when I eat, I have been trying to at least maintain my weight with protein and carbs. I have been a little lenient with my fruit and veggie intake, but I have also been eating them as well.

On the 12th, I did something I seriously didn't think I would ever do. Although I had thought about it, I got a tattoo on my chest; a small one on my chest of a red monkey, which was part of a symbol of a movie that dealt with mental illness and a lot of things I have been through to this day. I do not regret it. I think that I would have flipped out by now if it were a serious mistake. I am beginning to know myself better. I just hope that it lasts.

I finished my first college class in almost eight years and am pleased to say, I loved the professor and the fellow classmates with my heart.

### 28 May 1998

Right now, I am at Dawn's house. She and her baby are beautiful together. I have received my grade for the college class I took. I received a B, a 3.0. I now feel I can talk about school more freely.

I got my tattoo re-coloured and it now looks much better. I still get an occasional person say, "What is it?" or "Is that the barrel of monkeys' monkey?"

### 21 Nov. 1998

Wow, so much has happened in the last six months. While at school, I made a lot of friends, one of whom set me up on a blind date. The first day we hit it off and because there was a spare bedroom, two months later I was freed from the life of living with my parents. Not that it was bad, but it was becoming strained due to our own personal issues, which we were never able to express for as long as I can remember. I was, once again, becoming the black sheep. This is something that bothered my friend who vowed to get me out of there.

After I moved in, I transferred to a different movie theatre that was closer to home. I began to settle in. I created in time, a fortress that was my own, except perhaps, the cat.

I spent as little as possible, fixed the things that caused headaches and then made my move on the annoying things.

I painted the bathroom, put in new light fixtures, linoleum and shelves that were either oak or looked like oak. (I like the real thing.) In the kitchen, I bought burgundy panels, and mini-blinds for the main window. I added a table as my desk for my paperwork. I bought place-mats and a matching rug for the sink. In the living room, I bought green curtains with pullbacks and used the old curtain bottoms as a screen. I bought a matching rug remnant.

I replaced the outside light fixture that had been broken and out our own #6 in brass, because the other one had been painted over and looked crappy. I took scraps of carpet and somehow laid it down well enough you could hardly see the seams. There were other things like my ceiling fan in the kitchen, an $80 + fan marked down to $30.00 on clearance, if you can believe it. It was too sweet. I had to get it.

## 25 Nov. 1998

Today was quite rough. I worked the second shift under chaos. There was little leadership today. Rumors are going around that both the theatre will be bought out again, and also two members of management will be leaving.

I came to a conclusion that most of the world does not consider health or doctors appointments as a job. I say this because who would understand the hour or so in the exam room waiting for the doctor; she comes in we talk briefly. I go to my second appointment with my counselor. I have decided the best way to deal with this man is by, "Yup, uhah." I then saw my social worker. I had to do all this before work. It was not terribly busy, but the person I worked with did as little as possible. He did work, but only when he had to. And such is life.

The staff at both theatres is dwindling and no one appears to like their job. Why is this? A skeleton staff, few hours and no benefits, and a lot more grumpy customers reluctant to part with their money for concession that has doubled in price.

I miss my friends including my former mental health clinic, but my life was going nowhere and now as I am starting, new things are falling into place.

My beau is kind and the apartment is now home. The mental clinic is different than I had expected. I am not saying that the mental health clinic is wrong, just a lot different than I was used to.

**02 Nov. 1998**
**4:20am**

Here are my thoughts on a trailer someone is willing to almost give us—Well; it has not even been six months since I have been in this apartment. Despite oddities and rudeness of the now former tenants behind us, I love this place. It has just begun to feel like home. I was not ready to move into D's mothers house and I don't think I am ready to move now. I have not even seen the trailer, but this is not to say that owning our own piece of land was one of my dreams.

It is my thought that maybe out of the kindness of their hearts that D's mom or dad might let us store the trailer, let us fix it up and buy a piece of land with a septic and well, in this county. I am only just beginning to get established and thus it is my wish not to move, yet. I have been pre-approved for some line of credit and also have the credit union. Maybe we could make something go of this.

I know that what we have is not perfect, but to me, there is love and this is home.


**09 Nov. 1998**

Each breath we are
closer to the last
Breath when we breathe
our last breath. Will something
better and warmer take over?
All these November months
Maybe only God knows and
He they call the reaper
It is just, that in these days
We should live our life at ease
But are sent here to be tormented
Just to let it go? I think not.
Perhaps to steal a few of
Those moments to carry us through the later state.

Bliss is nothing more than a fantasy
Or can it exist on said moments
We can choose to love or we can choose hate
Can we choose happy or sad?
That is the unknown as it exists.

## 10 Nov. 1998

I am a son of an electrician. Not that it is a bad thing to be. It was an honest living, but it was also harsh. Harsh when the father figure scolded for not knowing the name of a tool. There was no memory for relation here. Today dreams are here. I trust D with my life. My new social worker is great.

## 15 Dec. 1998

Okay, I have had it with "The Man." The new manager at the theatre that replaced Jim, sneaks around trying to find fault with you. This to me is gross. If not sad.

I stopped in a convenience store to get gas and just like that I got told to come in for an interview. "The Man forgot we are people, not cattle. The popcorn itself is more here than I make in an hour, and that is a small. They have even added service charges wherever they deem fit. I've worked almost five years and have only received a $.25 raise to show for it. As for the calluses on my hands, I can't complain since it was my own dedication to the industry that I got them.

## 30 Jan. 1999

I believe I have a full time job now. For the first time in six years, I received a 40 hour check. Could this mean a status of function? I certainly hope so-- No more red tape and photocopies for the state that helps people reluctantly.

At work, I have had spats with the other person who also was promoted to "supervisor" and a few customers. One of which called me something to the effect of, "An idiot," respectably because I would not give him a dollar out of the register. I bit my tongue, but stayed strong in my beliefs. I asked him when he bought the popcorn if he wanted a soda or candy. He rudely said no. I later found a bunch of the dollar off med./med. Combo. When I asked him why he didn't present the coupon when he got his popcorn he said, "I forgot."

I bit my tongue and went on break. I wasn't really upset any longer however, although it was not raining, there was a rainbow in the distance. I took it as a good omen, from the powers that be. Rainbows always make me at peace.

I have been trying to keep in touch with my college professor. She was a wonderful teacher and was part of the wonderful experience at college.

## 24 Mar. 1999

The house is silent, except the whir of the ceiling fan and our cat occasionally popping his head out from behind a curtain.

I am doing well, and a couple of days ago I was hysterical and they wanted to commit me. I told them, "No, I don't think so." I told the group of mental health people that it was just a phase. And what do you know, I watched two movies and I am writing today.

It has been work, in my opinion that has caused me great strife. The manager, try as I might, has left me with little feelings for him. The assistant manager works his butt off and from what I see does about everything. He is real and has gone so far as to ask me if I'd like to go clubbing with him and some mutual friends. Unlike the manager, he has a human side.

As far as my job and the rest of the staff, I only have problems when the other supervisor is present. It is quite noticeable that she has some issues she needs to come to term with. She gets the soft-hearted guys and a girl here and there on her side and uses them to give me a headache, no make that a migraine.

The house here is beginning to wake up. A neighbor walks down the stairs. Another is vacuuming, as he does every morning. I hear coughing and an alarm clock going off. Some soul carefully walks back up the stairs. I hear a dog crying; it sounds like a baying wolf.

I have seen few movies to speak of. The last movie I saw, and thought worthy of my time, won a slew of awards. I guess five years in the business gave me a little insight.

D and I rearranged the apartment for a couch we will be getting in a few weeks. The couch was my grandmother's pull-out. I figured when I was upset that it might bring added comfort. To think of her sitting on the right side of the couch in their sun room. When I have visitors, they could watch movies with us and then spend the night if they cared to.

My dad helped me attempt to fix my car. My mother hands me a reasonable amount of cash and tells me to go get food. This was shocking. I did not ask.

I just called on impulse, the secretary at my former mental health clinic. We talked; I caught her up on things in my life. You know, I love her.

# Space, the final frontier

Well, I've written and re-written. I have even re-written what was written. I've tried to give an overview of life with a permanent illness. Somewhere in my journey, possibly in the Bible, I got that to know joy you must know sorrow.

I hope that I have entertained you with my writing and strange sense of humor. At least above all, I hope you found the humor.

At times it is difficult to smile as you go through painful transitions. Losing a loved one to an addiction, illness or any reason. Maybe that reason is still there. It just takes heart.

It now has been six years with this illness and you know what? I beat the odds probably ten times over. I am functioning.

I may or may not ever hold a steady full time job, but if I can get by, I should (key word) be proud of my accomplishments.

What can you do to help others? Maybe they are lonely, or ill. You do not have to give any more than acceptance. We all want to be treated as normal. We all want to be loved. Take a minute and talk to a stranger. You might find yourself taken aback.

What is left for me now? Space.